For Cathy at Christmas
with warmest regards

Joseph H. *illegible* '58

Generations
THE STORY OF ALBANY

Written by **DR. JOSEPH KITCHENS**
and **DR. C. STEPHEN GURR**
Corporate profiles by **JENNIFER HAFER**

A Study in Contrasts. Wagons loaded with cotton arrive at the gin. A model "T" Ford contrasts sharply with the mule-drawn wagons. Vanishing Georgia Collection, Georgia Department of Archives and History.

Generations: The Story of Albany

Produced in cooperation with the Thronateeska Heritage Center
100 Roosevelt Avenue
Albany, GA 31701
(912) 432-6955

By Dr. Joseph Kitchens and Dr. Stephen Gurr
Corporate profiles by Jennifer Hafer

Community Communications, Inc.
Publishers: Ronald P. Beers and James E. Turner

Staff for *Generations: The Story of Albany*
Executive Editor: James E. Turner
Managing Editor: Kurt R. Niland
Corporate Profile Editor: Kari Collin Jarnot
Design Director: Camille Leonard
Designers: Scott Phillips and Rebecca H. Carlisle
Photo Editors: Rebecca Carlisle and Kurt R. Niland
Production Manager: Cindy Lovett
Editorial Assistant: Jarrod Stiff
Contract Manager: Katrina Williams
Proofreaders: Angela Mann and Wendi Lewis
Publisher's Sales Associate: Darcy Rohrbach
Sales Assistant: Annette R. Lozier
Accounting Services: Sara Ann Turner
Printing Production: Frank Rosenberg/GSAmerica

Community Communications, Inc.
Montgomery, Alabama

James E. Turner, Chairman of the Board
Ronald P. Beers, President
Daniel S. Chambliss, Vice President

TABLE OF CONTENTS

Part I

Part II

Caroline Williams (left) and her husband William E. Smith were the original occupants of Albany's historic Smith House. See page 17.

PROLOGUE
Forces Near and From Afar

Braided in the course of time, currents fold to weave a river.
Generations surging past live their stories. . . and together tell its course.

Our history is like our river. It accumulates from many sources. Its power at times is concentrated, just as the flood of local events and distant wars have claimed our resources and shaped the lives of our people. In 1994, the torrential rains spawned by Tropical Storm Alberto swelled the Flint to historic heights, destroying neighborhoods and decimating the fortunes of those who bore its brunt. Like the Civil War, its known but distant causes seemed unlikely to menace the life of the cities in the path the Flint. Yet they came rushing down upon us in a torrent. Destruction and fear held sway for a while. It was replaced by a determined resolve to turn disaster into triumph. The city is now poised for resurgence and the 1994 flood has proved in many ways a blessing.

Beneath our land are other rivers: secret, silent aquifers that occasionally reveal themselves as "blue holes," jewels of nature—crystal clear, cold springs where the undercurrents have broken through. They are the visible signs of rich resources of water—perhaps the greatest in the world. In strata of rock formed over millennia, these layers of underground rivers suggest the forces, unnoticed in daily life, which accumulate and direct the course of our existence.

The land above, the water below: resources, power, and change. On the eve of the Civil War, Southwest Georgia had only been opened a generation earlier to settlement. In it were the great new cotton lands, ripe for slavery and agrarian capitalism. When the flood tide of civil war receded, cotton remained king in a one crop system that differed from slavery but little. White and black worked to master a market dominated increasingly by distant and unseen forces. Egyptian and Indian cotton brought uncertainty. Only the First World War brought relief, when local planters prospered from soaring cotton prices.

A new force arrived following this latest war. It was the Boll Weevil. This little insect cut a destructive path across the South. Despite more diversity in farming—peaches, tobacco, pecans, and peanuts were being grown—worldwide economic collapse in the Great Depression of the 1930's prolonged the region's recovery until after World War II. For more than a century, Southwest Georgia, like much of the South, languished in cotton farming and sharecropping. Then, mechanization, with its promise of efficient farming, drove many from the soil as machines replaced the work of men.

Slowly, new influences accumulate, dictating eventually that we must change. The River, ignored for so long, becomes a barometer of the quality of our natural environment. The system of slavery and its successors, racial discrimination and patriarchy—seldom questioned by whites—is finally challenged. Demands for equal access to public transportation becomes a litmus test for the just application of the law. Our hearts are divided. Distant voices cry change. Then, black aspirations give rise to the Albany Civil Rights Movement. Our African American community leads the march to racial equity.

Meanwhile, barely noticed, the domestic effects of wars and increasing economic affluence change the way we live our daily lives. Communications, automobiles, new employment opportunities, the democratizing effects of media, and medical knowledge all converge to transform the family and particularly the role of women. Social changes once took a long time to arrive. By the 1960s trends are reported constantly, relentlessly. Soon, a new world—full of promise but threatening with its insistent change—arrives.

What follows is a story of several generations of Albany's people. It is not a formal or academic history. Instead, we have tried to relate local history to events in the wider world while adding more stories to the tapestry that is the history of Albany. The generations we have conceived are arbitrary, but we hope they provide a workable framework for telling the story. And, like windows, will invite the reader to view another age and imagine what their own place in it might have been: an emancipated slave woman struggling for survival, a young boy entering the first school to be built, a soldier off to war, a woman becoming the first in her family to have a "public job," or a family caught in the tragic aftermath of flood or tornado.

An elaborate memorial in historic Oakview Cemetery. Thronateeska Heritage Center Collection.

This is a local history. It is not a story of great men or women, though some do approach greatness. Some influenced the world far beyond Albany. Nor is it about "society," a term that often sounds exclusive to modern ears. Religion, an essential element in the community's story, has been largely left out. It would be a study in itself and more than worth the effort. But we have not ignored the spirit of the people. We have sought to be inclusive of women and men, blacks and whites, children and adults, and to portray them in the context of their environment. And when influences from the larger world—unanticipated floods upon our banks—arrive, we look to find their effects.

Local history is hard to write, harder still to research. This work will replace none of the earlier efforts to record our history. A fuller history of our community will require many writings and many researchers. It can never be complete.

Much of what we tell is in the form of photographs and the reminiscences of local people, or is taken from the pages of local newspapers. We hope these things will encourage you to value the story of your family, treasure the records of your community and realize that history is also being made in places close at hand. History's role is not to preserve some golden age, frozen in amber, but to tell of the changes that brought us to this place and time. Even if we revere the past, we also find it filled with change, the one constant in life.

— Joseph H. Kitchens
— C. Stephen Gurr

· PART I ·

CHAPTER I

IN THE FIRST
GENERATION

*New Land
With an
Old Curse
1836–1871*

*The Hall family,
including
(left to right)
Robert, Joe Hill,
Hattie and Thomas
Hall; Susan Tift
Hall and Nelson F.
Tift; Glen and
Sam Owens.
Thronateeska
Heritage Center
Collection.*

*G*eorgia was founded as an outpost to protect the southern flank of Britain's American empire against Spanish incursions from its own colony in Florida. From St. Augustine and Pensacola, Spain maintained its claims to neighboring territories of the future United States through diplomacy and trade with the Native Americans. Even after the American Revolution, the Indian border-lands of what became southwest Georgia were the scene of a continuing struggle on the edge of empires.

The Indians who lived in villages along the Flint and Chattahoochee rivers are sometimes referred to as "Lower Creeks." A loose confederation, the "Creek Nation" may have been the remnants of a more popu-lous and complex society depopulated by diseases introduced by the Spanish expedition of Hernando de Soto in the 1540s. The Lower Creeks included Chehaw and Hitchiti tribal groups who had established villages in present Dougherty and Lee counties some-time after 1750. Old hunting and trading patterns were disrupted when the British colonized Carolina in the 1660s. Georgia's settlement nearly three-quarters of a century later in 1733 brought both conflict and interde-pendence for the Creeks in the South and Cherokees in the North, as Georgia traders and settlers moved into the interior.

Southwest Georgia Counties in 1880. Notice that the rail-roads out of Albany do not extend directly to Florida or Alabama, although the Brunswick and Albany line is oper-ating. From I.W. Avery, History of Georgia from 1850-1881 *in Thronateeska Heritage Center Collection.*

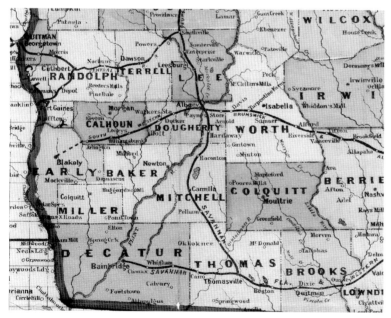

Following the American Revolution, the Creeks were, like many Native Americans, caught between a desire to trade and cooperate with the newly indepen-dent states and the effort to prevent the loss of their lands to the swelling population of Georgia. After the invention of the cotton gin in 1793, the land lust of Georgia's pioneers became insatiable. The Creeks were forced to cede their present day lands in much of south Georgia, a transaction that led to the Georgia

land lottery of 1820 and to the formation of the first counties in this part of Georgia. Whites began moving into the area almost immediately.

Florida, first under Spanish, then British, then Spanish control again, provided refuge and trade alter-natives that enabled the Creeks to play one nation's interests against another's. White traders were impor-tant emissaries of their respective countries, and some-times took Indian wives who were relatives of impor-tant tribal leaders. Because of Indian matrilineal social organization, offspring of such marriages were often influential and provided a cultural bridge between whites (Europeans) and Indians. One such marriage produced Jack Kinnard, the most important and wealth-iest of the mestizos in the Creek Confederation. His home and lands were located in present day Lee County (on Creek lands ceded in 1827) just north of Albany.

The Chehaw fought on the American side in the U.S.-Creek War of 1813-14, and later provided General Andrew Jackson with warriors in his 1818 campaign against the Seminoles. But their principle settlement, Aumuckalee (on Muckalee Creek in pre-sent Lee County) was overrun by a Georgia militia company while the village was unprotected. This dis-aster presaged the expulsion of the Native Americans.

In 1836, the last confrontation between whites and Native Americans occurred west of Albany in the swamps of the Chickasawhatchee. Remnants of the Creek Confederation living in Alabama, it is surmised, were moving toward Florida to find refuge with the Seminoles and were attacked by local militia.

In the early 19th century, many New Englanders saw financial opportunities in the South as well as the West. Southern towns in the former Indian territories often were begun as purely financial ventures. The region that now includes Dougherty County, already burgeoning with planters who needed mercantile facil-ities, was ripe for this kind of venture.

A native of Connecticut, Nelson Tift, came to Georgia in 1830 to find his place in the world. An active young businessman in Augusta, he moved to Hawkinsville, which was in those days a frontier town itself. Local businessmen offered to back him in start-ing a town on the west bank of the Flint River at the south fork of the Muckalee Creek.

Tift's leadership over the next fifty years made him not only one of the most respected men in the area, but one of the wealthiest. A Yankee entrepreneur rather than a cotton planter, he took an active interest in developing practically every kind of industry in Albany: saw milling, steam boating, flour milling, patent pharmaceuticals, newspaper publishing, meat packing for the Confederate Navy, and bridge building

and shipbuilding in New Orleans under Confederate commission. He was the driving force behind Albany's emergence as an urban frontier, a city of 1,655 people by 1860.

Soaring cotton prices and declining soil fertility on the old plantations drew investors and planters to the new lands of southwest Georgia, in particular to the area west of the Flint and the Red Hills section of what is now Thomas County. Fueled by profits and manned by slaves, this was one of the wealthiest agricultural districts in the state, indeed in the country.

Geography is destiny, someone wrote, and its location on the Flint River directed the history of the community from its founding. The Flint River was a vital trade and transportation link for Albany in the pre-Civil War decades. The Chattahoochee and Flint arteries joined at the Georgia-Florida boundary, becoming the Apalachicola River. In turn, it emptied into the Gulf of Mexico. At its mouth, the village of Apalachicola, behind the barrier islands, linked the fresh water traffic to the coastwise shipping around the Florida Peninsula and northward to the great ports of Savannah, Charleston, and New York.

The new owners of the Creek

lands that had been ceded to Georgia and Alabama found outlet for their cotton, hides, lumber, sugar, corn, and tobacco through the Gulf of Mexico. Cotton was the principle commodity shipped, exceeding a value of $7 million in the year ending in August 1860. For much of the antebellum period, Apalachicola was the third leading port on the Gulf, behind Mobile and New Orleans. Its success suggests the productive powers of the hinterland, of which Albany was an important collection point.

In the years between 1828 and 1861, about 130 steamboats were active, at different times, on the Chattahoochee-Flint-Apalachicola waterway system. Typically, side-wheelers built in yards along the Mississippi and Ohio rivers. The riverboats were flat bottomed and of shallow draft, having no holds. Cotton bales, hogsheads of sugar, and stacked lumber were shipped on deck. Cotton " boxes," square, barge-like vessels that were cheap to build, floated much of the cotton downstream. Some carried as many as seven hundred bales.

The river system was usually navigable as far north as Bainbridge year round. But toward Columbus and Albany, it was subject to the restrictions and dangers of low water, or low bridges in high water times. Snags, rocks, floating logs, and fires triggered by boilers allowed to go dry or sparks from the smokestack—all these might spell disaster. In 1845 alone there were three catastrophes in which boats were lost. One, the Viola, struck a rock just below Albany and sank. The hooked turn the river takes near the wreck site is today known as Viola Bend.

The central figure in the early history of Albany, Tift brought legendary "Yankee" drive and acquisitiveness to his task of raising a city in the wilderness. Actually, many farmers and planters preceded Tift into the area. Founder, editor, manufacturer, railroad pioneer and owner of Albany's first bridge across the Flint River. Thronateeska Heritage Center Collection.

Before, and to a lesser extent after, the advent of railroads, steamboats on the Flint Chatahoochee and Apalachicola Rivers linked the Georgia—Alabama Black Belt to the Gulf of Mexico and hence to the world's markets. From a postcard in the Thronateeska Heritage Center Collection.

As the 19th century came to an end, muddy streets, horse- and mule-drawn wagons, and cotton farming dominated the street scene. But the age of the department store, electric lights, and the automobile was fast emerging.

It was the coming of the railroads to the region in the 1850s that sounded the death knell of steam boating. In 1850, about 80 percent of the drainage region's produce reached Apalachicola. A decade later it had fallen by half. The same decade saw a decline in water levels because of a down cycle in annual rainfall. Afterward, the fortunes made in railroad construction, operation, and speculation dominated Georgia politics, as indeed, it dominated those of the nation.

Steamboats continued to work the Chattahoochee and Flint as late as the 1890s, some as floating piers from which to repair bridges and railroad trestles, or to dredge and remove debris from the waters. Former slave Bartow Powell held a federal contract to keep the river dredged and used the money to build his huge plantation holdings in Baker County. While steam power conquered the sea lanes after the Civil War, river boating remained alive mainly along the great Mississippi-Ohio-Missouri waterway system. The days of steamboats on the Flint live on in the imagination, evoking nostalgia for the romance and adventure of river travel.

Overland travel before the advent of trains was more than an adventure. Outings on horseback were rigorous. Even carriages left the sojourner exposed to the elements. Muddy roads, cold and heat, temperamental horses, and painfully slow progress turned even short trips into tests of patience and endurance, even into tests of courage.

The earliest train to reach Albany came in September 1857, opening a new world to the traveler. Although intended primarily as a way to ship cotton and other produce to market, the addition of passenger

cars made trips to Macon, Savannah and Augusta—and all points in between—easier and safer. As passenger cars were enclosed, heat added and dining and Pullman sleeping cars became common, travel would prove to be enjoyable.

Railroads came to carry away the cotton crop, but the real economic engine was slavery. Slavery in Dougherty and the other southwest Georgia counties was dense. By the 1860 census, 40 percent of white households owned slaves, while free labor—black or white—had all but disappeared. Many slaves came with overseers, not owners. Even though planters' wives enjoyed the social privilege gained by owning slaves, they often felt isolated. Mary Kendall, wife of a Baker County planter (in that portion that would become Dougherty County in 1854), complained in 1853 that there was only one white family within half a mile, "but any quantity of Negroes."

Nelson Tift hoped to solidify political and social unity where slavery was concerned by urging the state to grant inducements for every white family to own at least one slave. There seems to have been little need. Cotton prices doubled in the 1850s to about 12 cents per pound, increasing the demand for slaves.

Planters favored a gang labor system, utilizing large groups of men and women working under direct supervision by overseers or "drivers." Smaller farmers often worked alongside their slaves, preferring females who could do field work and who also carried the possibility of producing new slaves. But in general, the more slaves one owned, the greater one's importance. A majority of local slaves were owned by planters with thirty or more slaves.

Owners encouraged family ties and religion among their slaves. Some because it strengthened their hold, others simply reflecting the values prevailing in their own homes. More benevolent masters permitted slaves free time on Saturday afternoons and every Sunday. Slaves used such time to keep a garden or even practice a skill such as carpentry. Others visited neighboring plantations to spend time with family, to court or to attend church. At St. Pauls Episcopal Church, there were more black slave communicants than white. For trusted servants, unsupervised deliveries and errands permitted some travel. White visitors sometimes remarked or complained about so many unsupervised slaves moving about.

Iris Court (1856) was once the belle of Albany's pre-Civil War houses. It stood behind the Broad Avenue Federal Building and Post Office (1912) on the southeast corner of Jefferson Street and Pine Avenue. It was moved to Moultrie under the supervision of renowned classical architect, Edward Vason Jones. Thronateeska Heritage Center Collection.

William E. Smith's pass to travel about the South in his duties as Confederate Congressman.

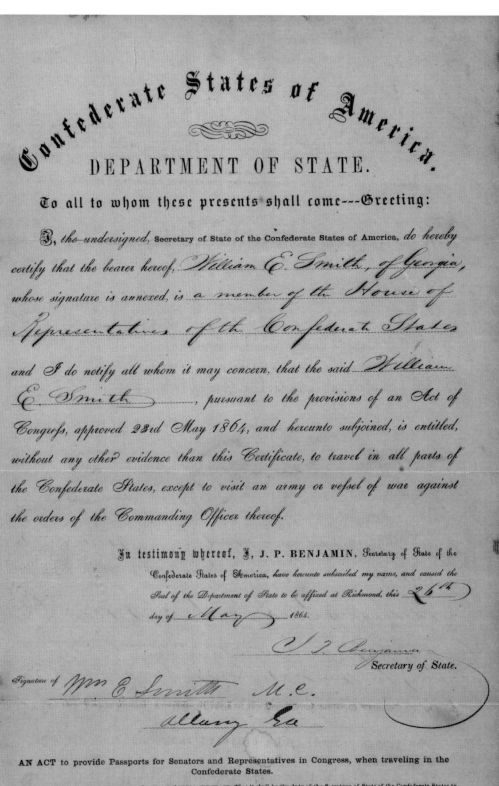

Planters profited by renting out slaves as brick masons, carpenters, and blacksmiths, as well as field hands. Horace King, at the time a former slave, was a master bridge builder, having learned his art to the extent that he built bridges across the Chattahoochee and Flint rivers. Nelson Tift employed him to construct a bridge across the Flint at Albany. The bridge house still stands today. King had been owned by John Godwin, who himself had studied engineering. Given his freedom in 1846, King remained Godwin's friend and collaborated with him on projects until his mentor's death in 1859. King paid for the creation of an elaborate headstone for Godwin, inscribed to reflect the love and gratitude he felt for the man who had once been his master.

The 1850s saw the rise of abolitionism culminating in Abraham Lincoln's election in November of 1860. Albany seemed fervently in favor of secession. The Albany Guards were formed in 1858 as a precaution. "Traveling abolitionists," reportedly stoking black discontent, outraged the *Albany Patriot*. The newspaper called for them to be hanged. As the secessionist movement mounted, toleration for unionists evaporated. When Albany bricklayer William Stewart implied he might decide to fight for the union, he was unceremoniously chased out of town. With irony, slave musicians played as Albany revelers marched to celebrate Georgia's secession in January of 1861.

In Dougherty County, several companies were raised, including the Hussars, the Thronateeska Artillery, the Albany Guards, and the Albany Independents. Sweethearts, wives, and sisters arranged picnics and concerts. Elaborate uniforms were fashioned of wool and adorned with gold brocade. Planters helped finance these volunteer units, and their families often provided officers.

Indeed, men from southwest Georgia have participated in every American war since the area was settled, including the ill-fated Georgia effort to aid the "Texicans" in their war for independence from Mexico in 1836. Georgia volunteers were slaughtered when they were forced to surrender at Goliad on Palm Sunday (March 27). When the Texans defeated Santa Anna at San Jacinto, it was to the cry "Remember the Alamo" and "Remember Goliad." The martial spirit seems always to have been heated in the South.

When war finally erupted following the Confederate bombardment of Fort Sumter, young men departed Albany from the newly built railroad station, a building still standing near Heritage Plaza on Roosevelt Avenue. Loving farewells were spoken and confident cheers followed them as they leapt to join the gathering thousands in distant Virginia. At Malvern Hill, Seven Pines, Chancellorsville, Gettysburg and many other struggles,

A daguerrotype of an unidentified soldier of the Civil War. Although the war did not reach Albany, its young men fought in the major eastern campaigns. Thronateeska Heritage Center Collection.

Albany's sons fought. Many died.

By the outbreak of the Civil War, the dye was cast for southwest Georgia. Its future would reflect its beginnings. A way of life was destroyed in the war; a spirit of bitterness born. Agriculture and the duality of the slave-master caste system would continue to shape the region's history to the end of the twentieth century.

The war brought changes to Albany. As the war went on, planters in areas threatened by Union forces "refugeed" inland, many to southwest Georgia. One estimate held that fifteen hundred "refugeed" slaves had been brought to Baker and Dougherty counties by the end of the war. Richard H. Clark, an Albany attorney, petitioned Governor Brown to allow some white owners to return home to reestablish order among disobedient slaves. Dougherty, Lee, Terrell, and Baker counties had become "simply one vast Negro quarter," he said.

Despite efforts by the state legislature to force planters into food production, the larger plantations continued to raise cotton. Cotton required intensive labor, and planters feared the effects of idle slave hands. Most of the cotton had to be stored because of the Union blockade around Apalachicola. No doubt, some cotton-laden boats escaped to sell their cargo in the North or abroad. Still, by the end of the war as many as 200,000 bales may have been stored in southwest Georgia barns and warehouses.

For those families whose men had gone to war, there were many fears. Even the wives of great planters had few legal and no political rights. Left with only overseers, their efforts to maintain order and continue production were difficult. Many appealed for husbands and sons to be returned home to deal, as they were accustomed to, with the complex organization of their plantations. Poor soldiers' wives fared worse. The *Albany Patriot* recommended that the city fathers pass regulations allowing the wives of poor soldiers to free range pigs inside the city limits. Moreover, several hospitals were set up in Albany during the war. Nelson Tift produced biscuits (crackers) for the Confederate Navy and also went to New Orleans to build a Confederate ironclad. He served the Confederacy as he had served his hometown, with the skills of the merchant, manufacturer, and builder.

Several scares not withstanding, the war never reached Albany. When Federal troops finally arrived in southwest Georgia following the Confederate surrender at Appomatox in the late spring of 1865, there began the emancipation of one of the most heavily slave-populated regions in the South. The path to freedom would be longer and more complicated than anyone at the time could have imagined. Reconstruction proceeded haltingly, first raising, then dashing the hopes of emancipated slaves. For whites, the fall of the Confederacy brought a social and political revolution to southwest Georgia.

Buoyed by rumors and hopes for the redistribution of land, the freedmen and their families faced emancipation with both apprehension and expectation. There was an initial wandering for many blacks as they sought to reunite their families. It is reminiscent of the migrations that accompanied the French Revolution.

White reaction is easier to understand if it is realized that following the war the black population of Dougherty County rose by a third to ninety-five hundred while the white population remained at about two thousand and this was in spite of the fact that fifteen hundred freedmen who had been "refugeed" to the Albany area left to go back to their familiar lowlands along the Georgia coast. From their point of view, uneducated, unskilled, and potentially violent blacks threatened planter security. Those who flocked to town were feared and the *Albany Patriot* advocated rounding them up and forcing them to work. The *Albany News* feared that radical politics might cause "every Southern homestead to be wrapped in flames."

President Andrew Johnson's conciliatory approach to white southerners ended when Republican radicals gained control in the 1866 elections and were able to override the President's vetos. Military rule was instituted in the spring of 1867 and under Federal protection, blacks began exercising their political rights. It was the harbinger of Radical Reconstruction in the state. Whites boycotted the election. This gave blacks a five-to-one advantage in voter registration and

A recent photograph of the Jones House on the northwest corner of Monroe Street and Roosevelt Avenue. Begun in 1855, this house was the ancestral home of Edward Vason Jones who undertook its restoration on 1950. Photo by Carolyn Seagers.

THE SMITH HOUSE

Construction on Albany's first brick home (right) began in 1859. It was for attorney William E. Smith (below right) and his betrothed, Caroline Williams (see page 5). With furniture from England and silver from Tiffany's, they began their life together in what might have been domestic bliss. But shortly afterward, the young couple's life was turned upside down when the Civil War erupted. "Tete"—a nickname from the french mon petite—enlisted and served as a Captain in the Confederate Army. Wounded, he lost his leg and returned home to stand for the Confederate Congress. His certification is signed by the Confederate Secretary of State, Juda P. Benjamin.

"Tete" later served in the U.S. Congress (elected in 1874), representing the Second District. These were still desperate times and reunion was still tentative. The future of the Union was at stake when the presidential election stalled into dead-lock between Samuel J. Tilden and Rutherford B. Hayes. An inconclusive outcome resulted in the creation of a commission to allocate the disputed electoral votes. "Tete" Smith alone of the Georgia delegation voted against the disputed electoral votes. To the disappointment of most Southern voters, the Republican Hayes was proclaimed the winner, receiving every one of the disputed votes. Smith did, however retain his seat in Congress, defeating carpetbagger Dick Whitely. Albany supporters were jubilant and formed a torch light parade to serenade "Tete" at the red brick house.

For his stand against compromising in 1876, Senator Robert Toombs said of him:

"The people of Georgia ought to build a monument to "Tete" Smith of purest marble, whose summit should tower among the clouds..."

inevitable victory in local elections. Blacks won seats in the local election, but failed to post the required bond. Philip Joiner became the first former slave to represent Dougherty County in the state legislature.

Still, the former masters and the freedmen came to the same trough: the land. Planters, deprived of their forced labor, were eager to negotiate contracts that would commit blacks to crop production. If freedmen returned to the land, vagrancy and the freedmen's flight to town would stop. Order could be restored. With a thin Federal military presence and a state legislature eager to limit the new-found freedom of blacks with harsh vagrancy laws, blacks were initially forced to accept contracts which at best provided accommodations and food for their families. At worst, they found planters unable or unwilling to honor their contracts. The two groups were locked in a battle of maneuver over workers' claims for adequate compensation and the planters' irresistible need for labor.

Reconstruction, while awakening many possibilities and opportunities, failed to provide freed slaves with land. Blacks, though freed, still needed work and a way to provide for their families. Out of these circumstances arose the system of sharecropping, by which blacks and poorer whites worked the land for a share of the crop, typically cotton.

A compromise, this system again made cotton king, shackling landowners to the one-crop agricultural system. The peonage of sharecropping was only one step removed from slavery for blacks, but the difference was an important one. It gave them greater control over their own and their family's life and work. For some, it opened a narrow window to wealth. Bartow Powell, an enterprising black, succeeded in becoming a wealthy Baker County planter with Albany connections. But, by and large, it was the families of the old planter aristocracy who persisted in land ownership. It would be their sons and daughters who would become the merchants and professionals in the growing city of Albany. They would profit from the enterprises waiting to be developed: cotton factoring, fertilizer sales, railroad development, warehousing, and dozens of other occupations. Nelson Tift and his descendants, leaders over the past century and a half are evidence of this.

Fortunes were still to be made on the land. Thomas A. Willingham became the wealthiest planter in the county by 1870. It is interesting that he sought the same solution that textile manufacturers did when

Nelson Tift built a bridge house when he built a bridge across the Flint River. He had the interior decorated by New York artisans and used it for theatricals and social events.

faced with surly workers. He asked the Freedman's Bureau official, General Tillison, to procure two hundred boys and girls to work his farms. Despite the collapse of Confederate bonds and currency, Nelson Tift survived financially as the second richest planter in southwest Georgia, even though about one-third of his wealth was lost because of the war and the emancipation of his slaves.

Much despised by whites, the Freedmen's Bureau officials enforced labor contracts and pressed the freedmen to work. At the same time, they attempted to protect the lives and rights of freedmen. O.H. Howard, an agent in Albany received a letter from his counterpart in Miller County complaining that the civil and professional people in town were always using sharp practices to profit off the uneducated freedmen, especially lawyers who seldom missed a chance to "make a dime out of the unfortunate one in the hands of civil officials." Other freedmen were harassed by white vigilantes, sometimes in the robes of the Ku Klux Klan.

Cotton production soared in the Albany area during Reconstruction. New lands to the East and South were opened to cotton cultivation. Colquitt County's

production rose by 1,000 percent as lowland cotton proved adaptable to the lighter soils, previously thought ill-suited to cotton production. Albany's rail connections made it the focus of ginning, pressing, and shipping the new bonanza in cotton.

The postwar era would see a dramatic change in another realm: education. Before the Civil War, there was not even a primary school system in Georgia. The "Albany Academy" was built in 1840 with proceeds from a new state "poor school" law ($255) and public subscription ($1255). But the school proved inadequate and did not meet Nelson Tift's dream of "a system of State Schools which, like the air, and rains of heaven, shall be free to all." As one would expect, this was a white school.

Children of planter families usually did not lack for tutors and their children went away to college or finishing school. Before the war, sons might be sent to distant schools like Harvard or Princeton, but this seems to have been less frequent than in the case of the coastal aristocracy of planters where easier transportation and a more cosmopolitan point of view prevailed. Young women were more likely to be sent to Bishop Stephen Elliott's school in Macon, or one of the similar schools rising in the Carolina Piedmont.

Every community of any size produced advocates of free public education in this era and Nelson Tift was a leader in this as in almost every progressive undertaking. Before the Civil War, students paid tuition unless "poor school" funds could be provided for those unable to afford it. The state made a great deal of money from the development of railroads in the 1850s and was well on its way to creating a public system when the war intervened.

Since the state Constitution of 1868, Georgia has never been without some form of public school system, though in the early years it existed mainly on paper.

The American Missionary Society in 1867 sent six women to Albany to begin instruction for blacks. Ostracized by local whites, they took rooms with local black families. They found themselves the butt of jokes and were jeered in the local newspaper. Even whites who favored education for the freed slaves objected to the patronizing implied by having "Yankee" teachers.

In 1874, the first free schools were set up separately for blacks and whites in Doughery County. The school census that year listed 394 white and 2,488 black children ages 6-18. The old Albany Academy was purchased for $5,000 to become the city's first public school. Two-thirds of the money came from public contributions.

In spite of the apparent cataclysmic consequences of the Civil War—emancipation, black suffrage, the advent of sharecropping, and the potential ability of free black families to determine their own destiny—there is a great deal of continuity from the antebellum period to the postbellum period. Slavery was abolished, but the freedmen fell into a new form of peonage called sharecropping. The "Cotton Kingdom," defeated in war, rebounded in southwest Georgia.

For twenty years after the end of Reconstruction, former Confederates and Democratic "Redeemers" would again rule the South, unchallenged politically until poor whites threatened to become politically active in other parts of Georgia and the South. Finally, the development of a public school system, begun before the war, was quickly revived and extended to the freedmen's children, though black schools would continue to be stepchildren of the system until the 1960s. In all these things, Albany continued to reflect those beginnings made in the antebellum period.

One of the most important elements of continuity was the immediate revival of interest in extending a network of rail lines out of Albany. From its beginnings, Albany eventually would have seven railroads by the 1930s, most of the connecting rail being laid in the twenty or so years after the end of the Civil War. In 1868, the south Georgia and Florida was rechartered after a false start in 1857. It was completed between Thomasville and Albany in 1870. The first passengers were Thomasville Episcopalians coming to worship at St. Paul's. Transferred to the Atlantic and Gulf Railroad Company, it crossed the Flint on a new bridge built over the river. This system later became part of the Atlantic Coast Line.

Before the war, a line had been built toward Albany from Brunswick, but only reached Wareboro. Under new charter, it was extended to Albany, arriving in 1871. Because of a shortage of U.S. currency, Brunswick and Albany issued bills in one and two dol-

The Dougherty County Courthouse.

lar denominations, legal as "charge bills." The ink was hardly dry when the railroad company failed and went into receivership. It too was eventually absorbed by the Atlantic Coast Line. Although started in the same period, a line approaching from Columbus to Albany was not opened until 1890. It would later be part of the Seaboard Coast Lines.

Nelson Tift, as energetic as ever, was the man behind the Albany, Florida and Northern that reached out to Quitman, Bainbridge, and Cordele. The Cordele link became the Georgia Southwestern and Gulf. Later, the Georgia Northern was built to Moultrie where it connected to the Atlantic coastline.

All this construction made Albany a transportation and shipping center on a larger scale than before the war. But again, this trend had preceded the war. Railroad construction—not to say corruption—became a national mania in the postwar era and Georgia's governors, along with many politicians in the state, tended to keep one hand out for free passes and the other ready to vote for more railroads. It was, ironically, this boom in railroad construction that encouraged the legislature to choose Atlanta after Milledgeville hotels and taverns refused to accommodate black legislators during Reconstruction.

Railroads, cotton, and schools, all vital to Albany's future, had survived the war. While building their own churches and nurturing the protestant Christianity learned in slavery, most freedmen could see little of promise in their worldly circumstances. Whites sought to reestablish the old social order while taking up the quest for progress. The dual nature of Albany and southwest Georgia had also survived the war. ❧

CHAPTER II

AT THE TURN OF THE CENTURY

The Tide Of Technology 1871–1918

Cotton wagons, sharecroppers and field hands on their way to the gin. With a touch of irony or symbolism, the photographer has included the Confederate statue. After 1901. Thronateeska Heritage Center Collection.

*A*cross a century or more they stare out at us with clear features. Through the exquisite glow of sepia, they seem more real than the color photographs we took yesterday. When photography came of age in the late nineteenth century, America began a love affair with the camera that has never waned. The power of those captured images make the late Victorians real to us. We can see their vitality, sense love when it is present, and detect some hope unfulfilled. Before the other media of communication and art, new technology first gave us photography.

It is through photographs that we feel we know those people of the late nineteenth century. There are only a few now who survive from before the turn of the last century. Those born since have been entertained, if not always educated, by the motion picture, radio and television. Only a small number now can recall the age of horses or seeing the mules drawn up beside the water trough. Or the first automobiles, the thrill of live performances on stage, or the divine Sarah Bernhardt's visit to Albany. Those who recall the wooden blocks used to pave streets before brick pavers were used are all but gone.

Another generation of the Tift Family. poses for a photograph. Asa F. Tift, the boy in the cart, and Will Wooten Tift, the smaller child, were brothers. They drowned in the 1925 flood. Photo c. 1905. Vanishing Georgia Collection, Georgia Department of Archives and History, Copy courtesy of Mr. and Mrs. Mercer Sherman.

Why do we look back to this age with such nostalgia? Is it because this was the last generation that was not ruled by technology? It is probably because the infant technologies of travel and communications look so crude to us: screens filled with herky-jerky, silent actors, crackling sound on gramophones, and automobiles that seem less spirited than the horses they replaced.

It is in this generation that we see the first awkward human efforts to come to terms with the age of technology. We find it funny and reassuring because now machines and technology can seem so menacing, so beyond our control. So it is with some sense of relief that we look back to the optimistic world of the turn of the century. We are relieved to see their pictures. Their enthusiasm seems exceeded only by their exasperation over the new Machine Age.

Also to remind us of the late Victorians, we have the remnants of newspapers, browned by light or stored with the microfilm technology that itself is cause for amusement, so outdated does it seem. Spotty at mid-century, more complete files become available as we near the twentieth century. And there are other

printed sources for history: promotional brochures, timetables, tickets, and menus. With the Chamber of Commerce idea comes the need to trumpet the home turf as though it were the garden of Eden.

In general, the march of progress in the South seemed to lag about two decades behind that in the Northeast. Even though dependent on outside capital to finance industrial development and transportation, Southerners strove to keep up. Or at least some did. Others continued, mired in cotton and sharecropping. Still, diversification came in the form of new crops and we will give up the past for the excitement of the present. Albany was determined to remain among the leading towns in Georgia. Caught up like other towns in the boosterism of Henry Grady's "New South" idea, Albany used every means to turn potential into productive change.

Progress was in the air in the two decades that sandwiched the year 1900. A 1910 pamphlet is typical of the promotional efforts during this period. It is entitled "Albany and Dougherty County: The Land of Opportunity." It lists the community's assets: cheap land, agricultural potential, good irrigation, churches, handsome homes, "decent" cottages, and industry. Later publications would refer to Albany as the "The City of Courtesy," "World's Pecan Center," and the "Artesian City," the last a reference to the much touted medicinal value of the heavily mineralized water that could be released in a steady stream from underground sources.

Between 1910 and 1925, the population of Albany doubled. In the dawning decades of the twentieth century, the black population for the first time declined as hopes were set on jobs in the city, or looked northward to the booming capitals of industry: Detroit's automobile factories needed workers, Chicago's shipping required stevedores, Washington cried for servants. But all was not well in this other world. Race riots, antagonism from other ethnic groups, and the rise of the KKK in the states of the Old Northwest—Ohio, Indiana and Illinois—bred racial violence and discouraged emigration from the South.

As the 1870s ebbed, and Reconstruction gave way to recovery, economic development became paramount. The ultimate benefits of redirecting the economy were not apparent at first. The move away from a white controlled, paternalistic post-slavery society seemed to demand a more formal response to everything, from education and transportation, to poor relief and governmental organization. Schooling, care of the streets, city government in general, and recreation—every public enterprise seemed to lend itself to the emerging professionalism of business.

The old existing technology of the railroad was

Although African Americans enjoyed greater mobility and some ability to negotiate better working conditions after emancipation, it was largely their labor that made the cotton crop possible. Two women spreading guano (fertilizer) c. 1940, a scene little changed since the 1870s. Thronateeska Heritage Center Collection.

mated to the newer technical innovations like electric power, telephones, and more importantly, automobiles. But, retarding every effort to exploit the new opportunities borne on the wave of technology, was the cash-crop system centering on cotton. Farmers—black and white, tenant and sharecropper, small independents and big planters—were bound to king cotton and his fickle rewards.

Coupled with the credit system that linked sharecroppers to crossroads commissaries, planters to wholesalers and banks, and the latter often to northern holding companies and financial conglomerates, a revolution would be required to free up the economy. Still, in other ways, southwest Georgia was like the rest of the country. It was becoming "urbanized." When paying taxes and marketing the crop were the only reasons to come to town, people seldom came. But by the 1890s the train station, markets, theaters, the Chautauqua, and impressive churches gave new reasons to visit. Ice cream parlors, bicycles and later the "movies" and automobiles accelerated the rise of Albany.

Not everything that added to Albany's image came as new-fangled technology. In 1881 John Porter Fort dug the first artesian well near Albany. By the end of the decade the public well at Broad and Jefferson

The Albany Guard Exhibition Drill Team. Such units were common in small towns and reflected the flamboyant style of late Victorian military uniforms, both here and in Europe. Thronateeska Heritage Center Collection.

streets in Albany was the major gathering spot for the community. In 1887, the city officially adopted this new phenomenon as its emblem, becoming the "Artesian City." So, one of the oldest of local resources became a key symbol of hospitality, hopefully attracting newcomers. The minerals of local waters were used to promote the healthful benefits of living here. Not coincidentally, mineral springs, all the rage in Europe in the early nineteenth century, became very popular among late-Victorian travelers. Then as now, Americans sought some simple, natural way to maintain or restore good health.

The *Albany Advertiser* was around as a source of information about Albany even before it became the "Artesian City." A rare copy of October 11, 1879, tells us much about both what was happening and what interested local readers. Commerce is of course the central concern of life. Doctors and lawyers from Arlington and Camilla displayed their business cards on the front page, a sure sign that the "big-city" newspaper was ending up under the noses of their potential clients and patients.

From as far away as Savannah there were numbers of ads for dry goods and home furnishings. The Albany House Hotel provided lodging for the "traveling public." Who was coming to town? Mr. Phillip Harris, "jeweler and watchmaker," for one. Mr. Harris would soon be at Welch and Mitchell's store in Albany for a visit. The Southwest Georgia Fall Fair of the Industrial Association would be in town the first three days in November, singing the praises of Atlanta newspaper editor Henry Grady's "New South Creed."

Both Macon and Thomasville invited Albanians to similar fairs, both a short train ride away.

Travel seemed to be foremost in the average person's plans, judging from the *Advertiser*. The Atlantic and Gulf Railroad brought travelers who left Savannah at 4:10 p.m. and reached Albany by 11:00 the following morning. These were still the days when horses and mules provided most of the travel power, with no automobiles in sight. There was public transportation in the form of an "omnibus" to "convey passengers to and from different railroads promptly and free of charge." What is an omnibus? A large horse-drawn wagon, perhaps even a carriage.

The press of the late nineteenth century provided some fairly concise news items: "Its Hot," "River Rising," "East Albany Quiet," "Lumber Very Much in Demand," "Business Dull." Such headlines were not followed by articles. They were the whole story.

Advertisements were, then as now, as vital as the news. Ads helped buyers find sellers and vice versa. J. R. Hilsman offered "dry goods, hats, boots, shoes, saddles, buggies and whiskey." Tailoring, dyeing, and cleaning were available from J. A. Rumbney. And politics were the bread and butter of the newspaper then as now. The *Advertiser's* editor advised to "Register to vote on the bridge question or Albany will suffer!" Mild fare indeed compared to the flaming press of Reconstruction times. But as always, it was the crop upon which every thought was focused, and in 1879 the *Advertiser* announced "a splendid prospect for a big crop." Fairs, horse races, brass bands and militia parades would all celebrate the arrival of King Cotton.

But not all was business. Life beyond the toil of cotton fields was full in ways long forgotten in later generations. And not even church should come between a boy and his natural instincts: "There is no getting over the fact that the average Albany boy actually gets more solid fun from a stroll out to the fairgrounds and down to the river on Sunday afternoon than from going to Sunday School," editorialized the *Albany Herald*.

In 1879 in nearby Camilla, the Evergreen Jubilee was being held for the ninth time. "Colored people have been celebrating the year of Jubilation each year (since 1870) and have raised over six hundred dollars," reported the *Advertiser*. Dr. J. B. Twitty gave the opening address at the recent celebration, calling for a day of pleasure, of liberty, of freedom from feeling and thought of the doctor bills, merchant accounts, lawyer fees and newspaper subscriptions." One wonders what priorities whites might have assigned to these concerns. At any rate, they sound very familiar to the modern reader.

As the twentieth century dawned, there had already been balloon flights (1889) and a bicycle craze (1890s). An opera house was built in 1896, a library association begun in 1899, and a Chautauqua Society organized in the 1890s. The Chautauqua movement became a national mania for a time in the 1890s. It combined religious instruction with continuing education. It also offered opportunities to attend cultural events and brought many of the great voices of American oratory to small towns like Albany. The largest Chautauqua auditorium in the state was built here, then torn down and replaced by an even grander Municipal Auditorium in 1916. Woodrow Wilson and Champ Clark came here. John Philip Sousa's Band performed here. The building even housed a library before Andrew Carnegie's beneficence brought a library building to Albany.

As the city felt itself less a frontier community and more within the "pale" of regular society, it was to be expected that new efforts would be made to regulate the "unruly elements." As early as 1885, Nelson Tift had urged the adoption of a law prohibiting the sale of intoxicating liquors. He and others felt there were too many saloons, too many drunks, and too many fights. Tift died in November 1891, but the prohibition movement won at the state level in 1907 and at the national level during World War I.

It should be kept in mind that the war on "demon rum" was a component of a broader effort at reform. Many of the great social reform efforts like the Women's Suffrage Movement, the anti-child labor movement, the fight to end tenement housing in the cities, and the educational reform movement spawned

FROM THE RIVER'S EDGE

"*My father said that as a young man, he remembers some men taking out two sturgeons trapped in a hole below what is now the Seventh Avenue trestle. He guessed they weighed over three hundred pounds each, and they sold steaks from them throughout Albany.*

Within the past ten years, the world's largest striped bass (52 pounds) was caught just below the Lake Worth Creek Dam. Prior to the Lake Seminole Dam, I can remember seeing mullet jumping out of the water as far upstream as Radium Creek. At this junction, Duck Wight caught a two inch long flounder (a salt water fish) that he gave to me, and I kept him alive several months in an aquarium.

As a small boy (ten), I joined up with two older boys and we spent days and nights fighting, trapping, and exploring on the river... These older friends were big strong, mean guys, but I liked them a lot. One was Gano Slaughter (since dead) and the other, James Henley, who has been with the Border Patrol for many years in California. I learned the river between Albany and Goat Island from these two. James' father Bub loved to poach deer and turkey on Pineland and Blue Springs (Plantations). I heard he was once seen carrying a deer on his shoulders across the Broad Street Bridge after the wardens cut his boat adrift on Blue Springs Plantation.

All up and down the Flint were remains of wrecked and burned river boats. They were usually covered with rocks and trees. When the river was dredged, the old boat remains were a great place to pile rocks, so they all looked like rock islands..."

A story from Jim Pace. Today we are not connected to the river, although a riverside park and biking trails are planned. Perhaps they will bring us back to the edge of the river.

by John Dewey, as well as the pure food and drug laws, all reached a crescendo during the decade or so before World War I. The same might be said of the religious fervor of the period, resulting in the great missionary efforts of the protestant churches. It is no accident that the Methodist Church was a leading force behind both prohibition and overseas missions.

When Nelson Tift died there were no telephones in Albany, but they came before the end of the century (1898). However, he had lived to see electric lights installed at Broad and Washington. Albany claimed to have the first Edison municipal incandescent system to be erected in the South.

Such progress is all the more surprising if one considers that there had been a worldwide agricultural commodities depression off and on since the Civil War. A bone-crushing depression that hit the country in

1893 sent cotton prices tumbling to five cents per pound. It was a year in which police chiefs and the rich all over the country braced themselves for revolution. Northern millionaires built retreats at Jekyll Island or bought plantations in Thomas County, sometimes actually needing an "escape." Banks closed and industrial jobs were hard to come by. Not surprisingly, hard times put tremendous stress on the fragile black-white partnership that was the foundation of the area's economy. The Populist Movement was an effort by farmers to build a political party to further their interests against the greed of industry and the corruption of the cities. Both of these had undermined democracy from their point of view.

In the days before there were Jim Crowe laws and before blacks were altogether driven from public office and the polling places, Georgia Populist leader Tom Watson attempted to forge an alliance between poor whites and blacks. The hardships of farm life and the depression of the 1890s had driven him to attack the privileged and rich. The Populists fared poorly among the cotton sharecroppers here and larger landowners argued that blacks would assume political control if ever given encouragement.

So Watson's hoped-for alliance never got off the ground. But its failure had a profound effect on Albany and all of Georgia. The very idea of full black participation in politics sparked the passage of laws disfranchising blacks and requiring strictly segregated facilities in education and in public facilities. Not that seg-

regation was at all new, but putting into law strictures on the political rights of blacks and imposing de jure segregation hardened the line between the races, postponed equality, and guaranteed the struggle that would come over integration in the 1960s.

Perhaps the most remarkable visitor to Albany at the turn of the century was W. E. B. DuBoise (1868-1963). The first black to receive a Ph.D. from Harvard, and an intellectual and a social observer of rare insight, DuBoise traveled to Albany from Atlanta by train. Here he found the "Egypt of the Confederacy," "the cornerstone of the cotton kingdom." A generation after the end of Reconstruction, he found Albany surrounded by another "little city of black people scattered far and wide over three hundred lonesome square miles of land, without train or trolley, in the midst of cotton and corn, and wide patches of sand and gloomy soil."

This description from *The Souls of Black Folk* is followed by one recounting his passage through south Albany:

"We passed the scattered box-like cabins of the brick-yard hands, and the long tenement-row facetiously called the 'Ark,' and were soon in the open country… The whole land seems forlorn and forsaken. Here are the remnants of the vast plantations of the Sheldons, the Pellots, and the Rensons; but the souls of them are passed. The houses lie in half ruin, or have wholly disappeared; the fences have flown, and the families are wandering in the world."

Carriages drawn up before the new Albany Hotel. Thronateeska Heritage Center Collection.

A MARTIAL SPIRIT

*S*outherners have a tradition of patriotism and readiness to fight when duty calls. Following the Civil War, the military defeat of the Confederacy brought a great sadness to many, both to those who fought and to the children of the next generation. Toward the end of the nineteenth century, the U.S. battleship MAINE exploded in Havana Harbor on February 15, 1898. Under an astonishing press barrage, Congress pledged the U.S. to a war to free Cuba from harsh Spanish rule, and the South's sense of duty swelled.

Americans flooded to enlist. Albany's young men were incorporated into the Georgia units, most of whom sat out the war in camps around Atlanta or Chickamauga. Actually, the war was over before very many volunteers in the U.S. Army ever came close to seeing action. Albany men had for years participated in National Guard training at bivouacs like Camp Northern. Notice that the men are dressed in "Yankee Blue" (upper right).

After the war, which was easily won, Albany found itself the site of Camp Churchman when the War Department moved three regiments of volunteer infantry from Kentucky to Albany to escape a severe winter and await mustering out. During the winter of 1898-99, over 3,000 men of the First Territorial, the Second Missouri, and the Third Mississippi Regiments camped along the south bank of the Kinchafoonee Creek (right, an officer poses for a formal photograph) on the Leesburg Road. They nearly froze to death when temperatures here fell into the single digits.

Big, rugged, genial westerners, these men were admired and welcomed, especially by local merchants. They marched to the "Blue" Spring at Radium and to the sand dunes for rifle practice. They drilled on the stubble of the open fields along Leesburg Road and posed for photographs under the live oaks. They had been itching for a fight. Instead, they were mustered out in the spring, having gotten no closer to Daiquiri or Kettle Hill than Albany, Georgia. The glory had gone instead to Col. Theodore Roosevelt's "Rough Riders."

Southwest Georgians no doubt felt the Spanish-American War gave some closure to the lingering disunity of the Civil War. The ranks of Confederate veterans was thinning by the turn of the century. These two factors made it timely for Albany to immortalize its fallen heroes by finally erecting a monument (see page 21) in 1901.

When President Wilson asked for and got a declaration of war against Germany in 1917, Albanians enlisted or were inducted under the new draft law to fight in Europe. Captain Garrett W. Sayre of Albany (lower right), in a machine gun company was one of the four Georgia brothers to fight with the American Expeditionary Force. The guns along the Marne were calling and a handful of men from Albany would be killed. No marker identifies the site of Camp Churchman. No Albany memorial recalls those who died in the Great War. The Confederate Monument is practically hidden from public view in the cemetery.

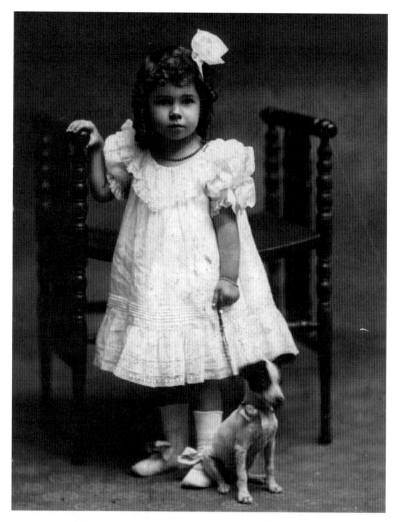

(left) Fannie Will and Her Terrier (c. 1900). The late Victorians idealized childhood and were fond of such sentimental compositions. (right) Photographers often used painted canvases as backdrops to provide an interesting setting for their subjects. This beautiful but unknown young woman wears the high neck, lace and wasp-waisted dress favored then (c. 1890). Photos by H.S. Holland. Thronateeska Heritage Center Collection.

Yet, DuBoise cautions his reader that it was not the white man of this generation who created this system and to bear this in mind in framing one's thoughts.

DuBoise is one of a handful of men credited by scholars with sustaining the black identity through the past hundred years, intellectually and spiritually. *Souls of Black Folk* is essential reading for anyone interested in Georgia at the turn of the century, though it carries the baggage of a brilliant, if occasionally overheated imagination as even his admirers feel.

The black community ran parallel to white society in some important ways. Meetings between races occurred mostly in the workplace, which was the field and the farm. Whites and blacks shared somewhat similar fates, tied to rising and falling cotton prices. It could be argued that whites, heavily indebted by the cash crop system, could only remain on the treadmill of credit, boom, and bust until their fortunes were lost. But surely, blacks were not sheltered by poverty from the cotton crop's vagaries. They faced the same fears of crop failure and low prices that whites did.

Some black businesses were either prompted by segregation or flourished because of it. Postal clerks were white, mail carriers black. Blacks owned and operated barber shops for blacks. Indeed, all personal care and grooming businesses became strictly segregated. Throughout the South, undertaking afforded an opportunity successfully exploited by blacks. Founded in 1900, Elliott Funeral Home will soon celebrate its one hundredth year in business.

In their desire to create separate religious organizations after the Civil War, blacks followed a pattern similar to whites, and Baptist and Methodist churches predominated. But because blacks were discouraged and later banned from political and civic roles, the church became not only a place of worship, but also a social haven, educational medium, and balm for the hardship they faced. Many of the now existing in-town churches were built in the period covered by this chapter (1871-1920). Prosperity beginning in the nineties would cause church building, as well as other public construction, to boom.

One other point. It has generally been thought that the rural black population in the South moved about very little in the post-Civil War era. From this notion followed the belief that limited mobility signified that blacks could take little advantage of their new found freedom to seek better working conditions or pay. Professor Lee Formwalt of Albany State University has done a detailed study of the federal census, property records, and tax digests to see if this idea holds for Dougherty County. He has concluded that there was a considerable and consistent relocation by blacks within the county and that each December they would often pack up to look for a better employer, better land, or a bigger share of the crop at harvest. So, the fact that they seldom relocated outside the county should not obscure the vigorous manner in which they moved about inside the county. It is likely that this phenomenon was repeated throughout the counties of southwest Georgia.

Little has been said of the poorer whites to this point. When the Albany Cotton Mill came to town in 1909, it provided the city with its first large-scale, twentieth-century industry, and the nature of work changed for many poorer whites. Former white farm families became factory families, with mother, father, and several of their children working in a new and impersonal environment, but one which provided steady, if mind-numbing employment.

The changing nature of work, the move from farm to factory, from crossroads commissary to company stores, and eventually to town merchants, forced locals into a new set of social relationships. Because blacks were barred from most of these occupational niches, the implications for race relations were ominous.

With the first decade of the new century also came the trade in nationally marketed products, such as Coca Cola. This soft drink, developed in Columbus and later the basis of a worldwide marketing empire situated in Atlanta, was originally sold only at soda fountains. First sold in 1886, it had become a national favorite by the time W. R. Haley established a bottling plant here in 1903. The plant carried a front page ad in every issue of the *Albany Herald* by 1908. Pepsi Cola provided competition for the "real thing" from its own bottling works. Both bottlers were still using horse drawn wagons and the railroads for delivery to outlying communities.

At the General Store (the old store, not the new chain), one could buy Kuppenheimer suits (again, the old, not the new version). The *Herald* also carried ads for "Piedmont Cigarettes," indicating that an old habit was taking on a new form as ready-rolled cigarettes created new markets, while addictions to cigars and plug tobacco remained strong in rural areas.

Mercantilism shifted to "ready made goods" and "store-bought food." The enormous productive power

Young Bachelors pose at a dinner party at the Wooten residence on Pine Avenue (c. 1915). Note that some are wearing tuxedos and white bowties. The masculine grouping suggests a bachelors' party. Thronateeska Heritage Center Collection.

THE TENANT HOUSE

"*All over the face of the land is the one-room cabin—now standing in the shadow of the Big House, now staring at the dusty road, now rising dark and sombre amid the green of cotton-fields. It is nearly always old and bare, built of rough boards. . . The majority are dirty and dilapidated, smelling of eating and sleeping, poorly ventilated, and anything but homes.*"

— W.E.B. DuBoise
after visiting Dougherty County (1903)

sow's ear, the state used its chain-gang system to create thousands of miles of new, improved roads in the state by the 1920s.

The first owners of automobiles were higher than average in income and education, frequently engineers, capitalists, and physicians. The first car to come to Georgia was probably one purchased by J. W. Alexander of Atlanta. Local tradition has it that Albany claimed its first automobile in 1900 or 1901, purchased by W.L. Davis. We know for a fact that the first automobile to be licensed by the State of Georgia was owned by J. S. Davis. The tag was a silver aluminum rectangle with black numerals and the letters GA to the right. No year appeared because the state did not anticipate annual renewals. By 1914, the volume of autos was such that the state, appreciating the opportunity of new revenues, began issuing annual and therefore dated "tags."

The Davis tag was the first of five thousand registrations issued by the end of 1910. Secretary of State Cook had promised to be impartial in issuing the tags, but the *Herald* reported that "An Albany auto will be the number one in Georgia, based on the fact that the Secretary of State promised the initial number to the Honorable J. S. Davis, and is holding it for him." The initial statewide registration shows Albany ordered 100, Savannah 600, Valdosta 75. Americus 40, Ashburn 38, Leesburg 18, Dawson 30, and Bainbridge 30. It is obvious that south Georgians took to the idea of automobiles easily. Just as automobiles came into more general use, an electric streetcar system was built in 1912 covering twenty-eight blocks.

Albany and Americus developed a kind of rivalry around the turn of the century and the fact that Americus only needed forty tags in 1910 delighted Albanians. Americus up until the end of the first decade of the twentieth century had led Albany in population. But the 1910 census figures showed that Albany was growing "15 times faster." From 4,606 residents in 1900, Albany had nearly doubled to 8,190 by 1910. The *Albany Herald* made much of the city's growth and vitality. On January 12, 1911, the paper reported that Albany was ranked tenth among Georgia cities in population. At that time there were only nine Georgia towns with populations in excess of ten thousand. Ranking above Albany were Atlanta, Savannah, Macon, Columbus, Athens, Waycross, Rome, and Brunswick. It is worth noting that only Atlanta and Athens on this list were above the fall line.

Baseball was another arena in which Georgia towns vied with each other for honors and glory. The "Albany Babies" were part of the South Atlantic (Sally) League and one of their favorite victims was the hapless Americus team, which was in the Empire

of immigrant workers in the North and farmers in the West worked a consumer revolution. In Albany, this expressed itself in new stores, particularly the new "Department Stores," forebears of the shopping mall with many departments—children's, women's, and men's clothing, linens and house wares—all under one roof, towering three, even four stories above the sidewalks. The age had found a new temple in which to worship. Churchwell's, Rosenberg's, and many others soon would grace the burgeoning downtown.

Old favorites like groceries, dry goods, and barber shops persisted downtown, along with drugstores, ice cream parlors, and the inevitable and ubiquitous hardware store—a Mecca in small southern towns. Here boys could find knives displayed, fathers ponder what tools to buy, and the family shop for cast iron stoves, plowline, nails, and for a time, buy gasoline for the new automobile—at first as much hobby as transportation. Was there anything worth having that could not be found in either the department store or the hardware?

Old names were joined in new firms like Tift and Mitchell Grocery, while E.R. Clark had "Automobiles for Hire" from Clark's Garage. He was the agent for White Steam Cars and Rambler Automobiles. No Fords had yet arrived by 1908, and there were initially few customers for the makes available. But, to repeat an old cliché, there was a big change coming down the road. As late as 1900, there were fewer than one hundred automobiles on Georgia's roads. Choking with dust in summer and sliced with muddy ruts of slippery clay in winter, Georgia's roads were a major impediment to automobiling, as was the proverbially flat Cracker pocketbook. Making a silk purse out of a

The Albany Normal School for Negroes evolved into Albany State University. Photograph by H.S. Holland. Copy in Thronateeska Heritage Center Collection.

State League. Interleague rivalries were common in the days when travel was so time consuming. Baseball achieved enormous popularity, nationally as well as locally, in the 1910s. And things were humming in the years before the United States entered World War I.

In the black community, a man who would be a longtime leader arrived in 1903. He was Joseph Winthrop Holley. He established the Albany Bible and Manual Training Institute. Through Holley's nurture and a growing sense of responsibility for providing "Negro" education on the part of the state, Albany Bible evolved into a state-supported college, first as one of the A&M (Agricultural and Mechanical) schools, then as Albany State College (granted university status in 1997).

Ten years later, in 1913, the *Albany Herald* announced that "moving pictures" were to be taken of the Albany community. Subjects to be included were to be "a run of the fire department," an automobile parade, "a panoramic view from the water tower," scenes of the power dam, the court house, the Albany Guards, and the local Boy Scouts. The film, it said, would be ready for viewing in about two weeks.

By far, the most devastating arrival in 1913 was the boll weevil that had marched its way from the Rio Grande to Georgia, wreaking more havoc than General Sherman. For the first time the one crop system of agriculture seemed far less appealing. Fields were raked and burned. Children were paid to pick the insects off the plants, and various poisons were tried. Plants were "painted" with a mixture of poison and molasses. Despite this blight, there were many who saw the voracious little insect as a blessing in disguise, pushing Georgia out of the rut of one crop agriculture.

Ironically, as the boll weevil arrived, so did mounting orders for cotton required by the growing armies of Europe as World War I got underway in August of 1914. And not only for uniforms. Cotton was used in

HIGH SCHOOL. ALBANY, GA.

munitions production, as insulation, webbing for shipping—the applications numbered in the hundreds. The *Albany Herald* seemed to back President Wilson's determination to keep America out of the war in Europe. But Wilson contended that America's rights as a neutral included the freedom for Americans to travel on neutral or belligerent ships in the war zone around England. And he insisted on America's right to sell to all the belligerents, though this favored Great Britain since surface traffic to the continent was all but cut off by the British fleet. So, while America's neutrality lasted, southern cotton soared in value and continued to do so after American intervention in 1917.

But the boll weevil had convinced many savvy and influential people that cotton had to be dethroned and a more diversified agricultural economy developed. The general flourish of economic activity before and during World War I also engendered a more adventurous and creative spirit in Albany. In this spirit, the community promoted tourism, pecans, and the immigration of new labor sources. Again, the natural beauty

Albany's first High School was built in 1908.

Washington Street, Albany, Ga.

A streetcar north-bound on Washington. Streetcars arrived here just in time to be eclipsed by automobiles. Thronateeska Heritage Center Collection.

A Temple of Mercantilism. By the turn of the century the age of the department store had arrived. Built in 1892, this building housed the Davis and Brown establishment. The electric and telephone cables were in place before 1900, although the photo dates from c. 1925. Thronateeska Heritage Center Collection.

Symbol of a New Age. The first automobile to be licensed in Georgia was to an Albanian. Here a driver proudly poses at the wheel of his automobile for a photograph on Broad Avenue c. 1912. Notice the trees in the median have been growing only a few years. Thronateeska Heritage Center Collection.

FEDERAL BUILDING
ALBANY. GA.

The Post Office was constructed in 1912 on the corner of Broad and Jefferson Streets.

of the area and healthy environment were touted as drawing cards for the area.

Although Albany never claimed that picking Yankees was easier than picking cotton, as did Thomasville, Albany's enthusiasm for promoting the virtues of the region blossomed in the founding of the Chamber of Commerce. In agriculture, Haley Farms became the largest orchard of improved variety pecans in the world. The remnants of the early pecan orchards are found in many Albany suburbs developed since the 1940s.

In September 1915, the local news reported "A Colony of fifty white families coming to Dougherty County." The article said that by December, the first of these "experienced farmers" from the Chicago area would be arriving. The *Herald* editor promised that they would be coming with "sufficient capital to make down payments on labor and to provide for their support for at least a year." The immigrants would settle on forty-acre tracts, but the location and details of the plan were still being withheld. The project vanished from the paper after that and we are left wondering if it ever materialized. But it is certainly reflective of the attitude of Albany's city fathers in those times.

There was a flurry in the construction of public buildings just before America entered the First World War, reflecting both the city's sense of civic pride, as well as the fact that these were more prosperous times. A hospital (Phoebe Putney, 1912), a new high school (1908), and an especially handsome YMCA building (1912) were built. Also in 1912, the new federal post office on the northeast corner of Broad and Jefferson was finished. Executed in the Renaissance style popular for public buildings in the era, it is perhaps the most beautiful public structure ever erected in Albany. Congressman J. M. Criggs of the second district, who

served from 1897-1910, was the author of this project and a plaque commemorating his effort still hangs on the first floor.

Worthy of note, Nellie Brimberry was appointed postmaster (or postmistress, old style) in January 1910 by President William Howard Taft. The first woman to serve in such a post at an important city post office, she won acclaim in southwest Georgia by working to get Post Office Department approval for pecans to be sealed and shipped through the regular mails. Ever since, pecan producers have benefited from the mail order business made possible.

The new and modern "Prairie School" style arrived in 1912-13 on the breezes stirred by the creative genius of Chicago architect Frank Lloyd Wright. It appeared when the Albany Passenger Terminal Company awarded the contract to build a new station to Richmond, Virginia contractor A. M. Wardrup. The plans were apparently drafted "in house" by the Central of Georgia Railroad. The existing station was replaced by a large, up-to-date facility with separate dining room, baggage room, and waiting room facilities all under one roof.

Completed in October 1913, one year after it was started, the station reflects the time in which it was built. The Jim Crowe Laws, still relatively new in the 1910s, dictated separate black and white waiting rooms with correspondingly separated restroom facilities. It remains today one of the few such segregated stations still standing. Capped with an impressive tile roof, set off by twin porta-cocheres and a little later approached on newly brick-paved North Avenue (now Roosevelt Avenue), it was the perfect marriage of modern art and commerce. Today it is home to the Thronateeska Heritage Center, Albany's history and preservation organization, and is undergoing major renovations at this writing. It will serve as a history museum and meeting facility.

1913 also saw the dedication of a new county courthouse, the crowning achievement of more than a decade of vigorous building and mounting civic pride as Albanians embraced a new century with enthusiasm.

Finally, Albany witnessed the opening of the Municipal Auditorium in October 1916. Replacing the Chautauqua Building, it hosted—then as now—some of the outstanding talent of the era. In 1917 an aging and infirm (she had lost one leg) Sarah Bernhardt, also known as the "Divine Sarah", recreated some of her famous roles on the new stage. That spring, the "Boy Orator" William Jennings Bryan spoke at the new auditorium. Of course he was at that point considerably more than a boy, but his "Cross of Gold" speech

Establishing a Tradition. Founded in 1900 the Elliot Funeral Home is one of the oldest African American businesses in continuous operation in Southwest Georgia, and possibly the oldest black-owned business not connected to agriculture. From Aaron Brown, The Negro in Albany *(1940). Dr. Brown was president of Albany State College in the 1940s. Courtesy of James Griffin.*

at the Democratic Convention of 1896 had made a national celebrity of him and he had been nominated for the presidency as recently as 1912, only to lose out to Woodrow Wilson. The new president appointed him Secretary of State. To this day he is referred to as the "Grape-juice Secretary" because, as an outspoken prohibitionist, he banned alcohol from State Department receptions. It must have seemed quite a coup to have him in so small an outpost of civilization.

Broadway plays visited the auditorium for years, and in more recent times it has served as home to the Albany Symphony. Beautifully restored, it is—like the Station, the Carnegie Library, and the Post Office—one of the few important downtown buildings to survive from the pre-World War I era. Churches, government, public transportation facilities, and cultural institutions all fared well in the era.

By the First World War, the technology as well as the tone of the twentieth century had finally come to Albany. In 1918, the Albany District Pecan Exchange was established and Albany had become the "Pecan Capital of the World." The Famous Candy Company (later Bobs Candies) opened in 1919, eventually becoming one of the most consistently successful and original enterprises to develop in Albany. And the comics, the next great "cultural" medium, had come to the *Albany Herald* by 1919, the same year a Ford dealership in the form of the M.C. Huie Auto Company was established on Pine Street.

From the first, Ford's Model T's outsold all other makes combined. It was indeed, the "Universal Car." With easy-repair design and interchangeable parts, the Ford was exactly what Georgians needed. In its wake would follow gas stations, tire stores, auto parts stores, auto insurance agencies, paint and body shops, and the inevitable tourists caught up in the Florida boom of the 1920s.

The machinery of the technological tide was in place in southwest Georgia by 1918. Its name was FORD. And with Henry's little black machine also arrived a far-reaching revolution in manners and morals, subjects each deserving a great deal of study in their own right. Accelerated by the World War, social change was in the wind as Albany entered the "Roaring Twenties." ❧

CHAPTER III

IN TIMES OF TROUBLE

Remembrances of War and Peace 1918–1945

The Hall family, part of a small group of middle-class African Americans in Albany in the 1930s. Left to right: the father, Henry R. Hall; son, Richard W. Hall; mother, Annie May Finley Hall; and son, Jack Finley Hall. Richard was one of the Tuskegee Airmen.

hey are a special breed, those men and women who knew the Depression and the Second World War. Raised in adversity and tested in war, they were the most likely of heroes. Their generation bridges two dramatically different worlds. In sacred tones their grandparents told the stories of vanished ways of life, of slave days and farm life, of the "Lost Cause" and the miseries of sharecropping. Many of this new generation would live past the end of the century. They lived longer than any generation before them. Their world was defined by unprecedented prosperity. Yet, there was also a painful new awareness of poverty.

Our nostalgia for their age is strong. We replay their memories as though they were our own: silent movies, gaunt faces in Depression-era photographs, B-25 Bombers with gorgeous girls painted on their noses, Glenn Miller's music, and studio photographs of men in uniform. Born during or shortly after the war, we were our parents' life insurance in an age of uncertainty, a way to survive even if one's beloved did not come home from the war. These things we keep unchanging in the place where memories stay.

For much of its history, Albany looked to the Flint River for transportation and adventure. By 1920, a new Broad Street Bridge spanned the waters. It might as well have reached across two generations as well. Albany in the new era of the twenties now had a

In spite of the boll weevil, cotton continued to be a central feature of Albany's economy long after the turn of the century. Gins and warehouses employed many blacks, especially at the menial tasks of loading the heavy bales of cotton.

hydroelectric power plant, a symbol of the age of electricity. New industries would be spawned while others like the cotton mill would adapt to this new source of power. Electrical appliances would become popular as electricity was installed in homes.

There were new jobs for some. The Famous Candy Company (later Bobs) held promise for the future. Pecan production added diversity. Trees might just as well fill the old cotton fields since the boll weevil had made cotton farming more precarious than ever. Peanuts were becoming popular among farmers. Few had tractors, but surely many dreamed of owning one.

Beneath this sheen of prosperity, blacks could see little change in their lives. Many left. In 1920, for the first time, the white population rose to one-third of the total. Urbanization was also reflected in the census. The city and county were in a dead heat in 1910. By 1920, the city had passed the county. In the years 1910-1930, the city's population grew by 215 percent, while the county's declined by a third. Black sharecroppers harvested about 40 percent of the crops in the region in 1930. About 75 percent of the crops were harvested by black and white sharecroppers, a sure sign of a broad base of rural poverty that cut across racial lines.

Such middle class as there was, was mainly white. However, there was a small black middle class largely

made up of a few dozen successful farmers, business people, professionals, educators, and ministers. Of 352 black-owned businesses in 1945, 159 were owned by women, a surprising figure in an age before opportunities for women to acquire business skills were not good and start-up capital was hard to come by. In the same era, 13 black physicians practiced in Albany.

South Central Albany had emerged as the black commercial district even before the 1920s. It was known as the Harlem business district. It was the heart of a larger black residential district south of Oglethorpe, bound by Monroe Street on the west, the Flint River to the east, and Cotton Avenue to the south. Like many cities its size, Harlem would soon have a motion picture theater, the Ritz, which opened in the 1930s. On the east side of the 200 block of South Jackson was a two-story building that housed the Knights of Pythias, a fraternal organization. Below was the office of the *Albany Enterprise*, the city's first black-owned newspaper. The Masons met nearby in the building that now houses the *Southwest Georgian*, also a black-owned newspaper.

Best known of the businesses in the district was Joe Malone Sr.'s Alcazar Club. Built before the war, it was a dance hall, but in the 1920s doubled as a basketball court for the black high school. The school had no basketball court at the time. Popular through the World War II years, the club was demolished in the 1950s. For blacks, as for whites, the era of night clubs would dry up in small towns with the advent of television.

There was also some ethnic diversity as earlier Jewish immigrants established themselves as merchants and businessmen. Their wives became advocates of a higher culture, grounded in European traditions.

Albany in the interwar years continued to be a railroad center. By the late twenties, Union Station was a stopover for more than thirty passenger trains every day. Yet, ironically, much of the era's prosperity rested not on the railroad, but on the automobile. Eventually, gasoline-powered trucks would wrench much of the traffic away from the smaller rail lines, and passengers would choose the convenience of traveling either by bus or their own automobiles rather than the train.

The term "plantation life" took on a somewhat different meaning in the 1920s as wealthy northerners began developing shooting preserves in the region. Cheap land and an agreeable climate had attracted such "Yankee" owners as early as the 1880s to the Thomasville-Tallahassee "Red Hills" region. There were strong Standard Oil and Cleveland, Ohio connections among owners of the pine-forested plantations of the Thomasville-Tallahassee region. This was true in Albany to some degree, and by the 1970s there were about nineteen such northern-owned preserves in the Albany area.

On the plantations, the Bob White Quail was the prince of game birds and around him circled the traditions of fine shotguns, matched mules pulling hunting wagons, top-caliber field dogs, and white liveried attendants who sometimes served elegant meals in the field. Howard Melville Hanna, brother of senator and industrialist Mark Hanna, had a place near Thomasville called "Melrose." His children and grandchildren would later develop their own places as well. At one time there were eleven first cousins of the family who owned plantations near Thomasville. Mary Haskell Hunter, a granddaughter, developed a place near Albany. From Cleveland also came Horace Sheppard,

Walter C. White, Charles Elms, and B.C. Goss. Of course it was Robert W. Woodward of Coca Cola fame, owner of Ichuaway Plantation, who was best known to locals.

Plantation life today is much changed over what it was in the pre-World War II era, but its focus on sporting dogs, hunting, and wildlife gives our area a distinctive flavor. Some of this ambience is captured in Sonny Sammons novel *The Keepers of Echowah* and in the photographs of Hank Margeson published in *Quail Plantations of South Georgia and North Florida*. The Fall Feather Classic benefit brings celebrities to Albany every year to whet the shooting appetites of locals, although few here have ever actually enjoyed the thrill of shooting in the grand plantation style or attended the Georgia-Florida Field Trials where the best dogs of the season are tested and their owners and handlers are rewarded with prizes.

For most Albanians, excitement was provided by stories in the *Herald*. In 1920, the paper provided vicarious thrills to break the tedium of the routine of life in southwest Georgia. Real-life, lurid tales of murder and disaster, lynching and mayhem suggest that public taste changes little. The KKK had been revived in Atlanta in 1915, following the release of W.D. Griffith's classic movie *Birth of a Nation*. It depicted the old Reconstruction-era Klansmen as knights of virtue and reinforced many of the racial stereotypes

that still plague us. Life had imitated art.

At the Liberty Theater in 1920, Marguerite Clark was starring in *Easy to Get* and cowboy Tom Mix was shooting the rustlers in *Cyclone*. Nearby, *The Forbidden Woman* was showing. The *Roaring Twenties* were roaring silently on the screens of movie houses and providing sex and violence in the two genres of film that never die: the good girl gone astray and the steely-eyed cowboy fighting injustice on the western frontier.

As Easter 1920 approached, the papers advertised seasonal finery, straw hats, and forty-nine dollar men's suits from the Levinson Company. Dolly Demple ready-mix flour was touted for the cook. Franklin, Essex, and Hudson automobiles were advertised for the well to do, while for the average man, Ford still offered the Model T, as unexciting as it was durable.

Local dealers were only the small end of the pipeline of a mammoth industry that had risen in the cornfields of Indiana, in the Ohio heartland, beside Pennsylvania's steel mills, and most of all in Detroit. Albany's list of dealers included Thad Huckabee (Hudson, Essex, and Packard); Huie Ford, distributors also of Lincoln and Fordson Tractors; Lambe Automobiles; W.C. Holman's Studebaker and Cadillac; and, lastly, Consolidated Garage (Buick and Franklin). Related businesses included Garretts Garage and Oil Company, and Hood Tires. While profits were to be

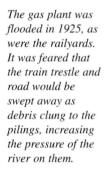

The gas plant was flooded in 1925, as were the railyards. It was feared that the train trestle and road would be swept away as debris clung to the pilings, increasing the pressure of the river on them.

VIVIAN BALES FAISON
DANCER ON A MOTORCYCLE

Miss Vivian Bales was an adventurous young dance teacher living in Albany in 1929 when she conceived of the idea of becoming the first woman to cross the country driving a motorcycle. She wrote the Harley Davidson factory and the firm agreed to help with her arrangements and expenses.

First, she went to Augusta to attend a national Chief-of-Police Convention. There she met many of the officers who would smooth her way and keep an eye out for her safety. So began her odyssey. She drove northward through Atlanta, Columbia (S.C.), Washington, D.C., New York, Ontario, Detroit, Chicago, Indianapolis, and back home through Chattanooga and Atlanta.

During her 5,000-mile journey, she says she took along her dancing clothes and was invited to perform on several occasions. Asked if she had been inspired to do this by Charles Lindbergh's recent flight across the Atlantic, she replies, "No, I just wanted to do it and there wasn't much to do in Albany." She lives today in a house furnished with pieces she built. She continued to teach dance to youngsters for years and designed and sewed

many dance costumes. An avid gardener, she sings in the church choir and continues to sew. Rummaging through her collection of articles and photographs, she remarks, "About every ten years or so, the Herald comes out and does a piece on me and my ride across the country." She adds enticingly, "You know, I knew Jack Dempsey, the fighter." And therein lies another story. Photo courtesy of Vivian Bales Faison.

made, the great fortunes that grew from automobile production remained north of the Mason-Dixon Line. The same was true of the oil industry centered in Cleveland and dominated by John D. Rockefeller.

Where money was scarce and desire great, credit—that great American leveler—closed the gap. By 1929, installment purchasing in the United States had reached six billion dollars per year. New electric appliances, especially refrigerators, and other "little luxuries" made for most of the rush to buy on "time." Ninety percent of all pianos, sewing machines, and washing machines were bought on credit, as were 80 percent of the vacuum cleaners, radios, and refrigerators, 70 percent of furniture sales, and 60 percent of new auto purchases.

For those who, by imagination or advantage, could gain a foothold in this part of the world, there were opportunities. Joel Thomas Haley (1881-1956), who grew up in Marietta and Chattanooga, was one such

person. After attending Emory in Atlanta and Henry College in Virginia, he worked his way up in a Chattanooga bank, cataloging a wealth of knowledge about the banking business in his head. He moved to Cuthbert in 1912 to begin operating a Coca Cola bottling plant. When Prohibition came along, it gave a boost to his business. Coca Cola was said to contain some addictive substance (in addition to sugar and caffeine, that is).

With money earned from Coca Cola, he built up sizable land holdings, especially pecan orchards. With his brother, W. Banks Haley, he worked with new varieties, methods of cultivation, and marketing strategies until Haley Farms became the largest farm in the world to grow improved-variety pecans. He became a leader in the regional growers' association. In 1928, the two brothers began the City National Bank (later First State Bank and Trust Company, now Regions) just in time for the onset of the worst depression in

Radium Springs was considered to be one of Georgia's Seven Natural Wonders. Developed as a tourist attraction in the 1920s, it lost out to Florida's wonders but became a popular swimming and dining place for locals. Destroyed by fire and damaged by floods, the rebuilt Casino has been the object of unsuccessful efforts to revive it. Still, it remains the most recognizable of Albany's sites and one around which many pleasant memories are centered.

American history. Through conservative management, the bank survived and Haley's influence spread as he became a director on regional bank and railroad boards.

In some ways, Haley was representative of a type that has succeeded in Albany. He came from elsewhere. He showed an acquisitive disposition and a penchant for business early in life. He also had an education that placed him in a tiny minority—an elite, in fact—before he began. Whether by genius, accident, or both, he invested his talents and money in consumer sales franchises (Coca Cola and later automobiles), just as the consumer sales revolution exploded. Of course, no one at the time could have known how these would fare over the long haul.

In other families, sorry land, poor crops, low farm prices, and a diet of side meat and greens produced different results. The grim realities of rural life in the 1920s were much as they had been in any decade since 1870. On the land still plowed by mules and on roads where wagons were more common than automobiles, a traveler might see the vacant-eyed men and women whose world included hook worms, malnutrition, and a hopeless repetitiveness. Black and white, they were

children of the dust. Victims of ignorance and neglect, they were championed in song, photograph, and story until the conscience of the nation was aroused in the New Deal Era of the 1930s.

White southerners still feel compelled to explain to their northern friends that Erskine Caldwell's hilarious and searing depiction of poor whites in the play "Tobacco Road" (later made into a movie in the 1950s) was a wild exaggeration. But the world known to rich and poor in the 1920s was about to change in ways few expected. A debilitating depression lay ahead. And by the end of the 1930s, the coming war in Europe would reshape the lives of all.

"Summertime, and the livin' is easy," was evidently written by someone whose knowledge of the South came from reading romantic poetry. Nor had he ever heard of gnats, those minuscule insects that swarm around people's and animals' faces in the southwest Georgia summers. And they certainly did not comprehend that summer brought noonday temperatures in the nineties, or nights so hot that sleep was often impossible. Sparks Hardware advertised in 1920 that Emerson Fans could be had for from $24.00 to $38.50. It undoubtedly would have seemed strange to visitors from other climes to see people sitting outside on the porch at night with the fan running and a damp handkerchief draped over their faces, an early form of air conditioning.

Convenient technologies affected women's life in the home. In fact, credit consumerism produced a revolution. Madison Avenue snake-oil and local door-to-door salesmen, as well as popular magazines, created a new "housewife" whose task it was—if ads were to be believed— merely to preside over her staff of vacuum cleaners, washing machines, and various other specialized electrical appliances.

Women's consumer power brought new women's magazines into being, as well as many romance magazines and romantic soap operas on the radio, as advertisers searched for ways of influencing the buying decisions of the homemaker. The *Albany Herald* began a weekly "Women's Interest" page that consisted largely of news from Hollywood and love stories. Combined with the movies, these were powerful influences in shaping the stereotypes of women that had become so powerful by the 1950s and have been the subject of so much impassioned rhetoric since.

The old pattern of press coverage for women strictly in their roles as church, garden, DAR and UDC members was passing. One local woman, Vivian Faison, made national news when she rode her Harley-Davidson motorcycle across the United States in 1929, a feat that perpetuated the string of "firsts" recorded by women between the wars. Still, it was their importance as consumers that inspired the expensive color ads in national magazines for exotic patterns of linoleum, tile baths, and appliances.

The whole world shrank appreciably in the 1920s. Growing news coverage, wire services, and the radio accomplished this. Images from remote parts of the world were at hand in *National Geographic* and *World's Work*. Photojournalism was coming into its own. In the *Herald*, there was a full page photo-feature called "Camera News," filled with stars, celebrities, and excitement. Charles Lindbergh's solo Atlantic flight to Paris in 1927 was reported there. In an age dominated by technology, Americans saw "Lucky Lindy" as an heroic "lone eagle" whose accomplishment reasserted the values of individualism and personal courage.

Tragedy garnered enormous coverage then as now. Two local disasters shook the community between the wars: the Flood of 1925 and the Tornado of 1940. The first of these was one of many recurring floods along the Flint. "Harrison's Freshet," so-called because it coincided with that president's one-month tenure in the White House in 1841, apparently flooded much of Baker County, which then included Dougherty. Of

course, the population was small then and not focused along the Flint.

The Flood of 1925 reached about 36 feet—comparable to the flood of 1998. Farm animals were afloat, and low-lying areas north and south of town were especially hard hit. Bridges and trestles were threatened. What really turned this show of nature's power into a tragedy, however, was that it took the lives of two local young men, Will and Asa Tift, both descendants of Nelson Tift. They were experienced outdoors men and Will was an Olympic-class swimmer. In the heroic manner of young men of their era, they decided to pit themselves against nature by canoeing in the raging waters. Caught in a vortex that pulled them straight down, both were drowned. Initial searches for the bodies were frustrated by the flood. Mercer Sherman, the boys' cousin and adoptive brother, came home from the University of Georgia by train. In 1996, he told the story of his sad return. According to Mr. Sherman, the engineer was afraid to cross the railroad trestle. Debris and tree limbs had collected in the trestle braces, increasing the pressure at the top of the bridge. Would it bear the weight of the train? After

The St. Nicholas Hotel on North Washington Street was damaged as the tornado of 1940 approached the train station from the Southwest. Amazed pedestrians wandered the streets later in the day, inspecting the damage.

Behind the St. Nicholas Hotel the Georgia Southern Railroad's facilities were devastated. Thronateeska Heritage Center Collection.

some hesitation, the engineer disconnected the passenger cars and began pulling them across one at a time.

Mr. Sherman joined the search for his brothers' bodies. But it was days before the boys' bodies were found, despite around-the-clock vigils at bridges below Albany. Of course, the family's several branches have survived and prospered, but there remains a tragic tone in the story of these boys' deaths that has lingered in the telling over the years. They were clean-cut examples of young American manhood, strong and popular. Their deaths shook the city.

During World War I, the country had experimented with Daylight Saving Time—that is, longer afternoons, shorter mornings. When the subject was debated locally, the *Herald* conducted a survey under the banner "Does Albany Want Daylight Savings Time?" The poll was conducted just as the city council was debating this issue, locally referred to as "Fast Time." On April 13, the results were published: Albany repudiated "Fast Time" 687 to 321. The city council concurred the next day.

Slow to accept change emanating from "outside," Albany and southwest Georgia were well ahead of trends when it came to economics. Long before the Depression turned up on the national doorstep in 1929, Albany's economy went sour. In the fall of 1923, local papers carried the painfully obvious news that the boll weevil had ravaged the cotton crop. Land that had produced a thousand bales in 1903 could yield little more than a hundred in 1923.

There seems to have been greater prosperity in town than on the farm. During the 1920s, a new high school, Albany High, was built on Jefferson Street.

The Albany Theater also became the city's first steel-framed building. Before the end of the decade, Madison High opened as the first secondary school for "Negroes." Albany High would win state baseball and football championships in the early 1930s.

Most reflective of the spirit kindled by the new Chamber of Commerce (in its new building on Oglethorpe since 1921) was the effort to sidetrack some of the Florida tourists, south bound "Tin Can" motorists. Known as Blue Springs until 1925, they were re-christened Radium Springs. Baron Collier, a promoter, developed an inn and casino and "Skywater Park" across the street. Though close to the hearts of local whites in all its subsequent reincarnations, Radium Springs never drew a reliable string of tourists. This in spite of the fact that it was for many years referred to as one of the "Seven Natural Wonders" of the state. By any standards, it still is, and it reveals in beautiful form the nature and extent of our underground water resources.

The onset of the national depression set off a falsetto chorus of optimistic articles about diversification and industry. One September issue of the *Herald* carried a full page describing "Products Made in Albany." The list was unfortunately short: Reynold's Boxes, Rucker's Bread, Bobs Candy, Lasca Cigars (hand rolled), Pace Bricks, Flint River Bricks, Lilliston Harvesters, Flint River Mills, Purity Ice Cream, and Plant Peanut Meal. For Albany, as for much of the South, the Depression started early and ended late. But Albany's claim to diversity of production held some truth and a hope for the future.

On the pages of the *Herald* in the fateful fall of

The railroad passenger terminal lost most of its clay tile roof in the tornado of 1940. Its north porte cochere was blown off and the two original dormers disappeared entirely. The dormers were never replaced and the porte cocheres were rebuilt with only half their original overhang. Today the station is part of Thronateeska Heritage Center.

1929, was an account of a dangerous rain storm with high winds. At the movies, though, life went on as usual. Clara Bowe and Harold Lloyd were playing in a talking movie—an innovation many brushed off as merely a fad. In sports, Yale was to play the University of Georgia in Athens and local fans could buy a round-trip ticket for a special excursion train to take them to the game. The cost was $7.67 each. Such special excursions were always popular with small town schools, churches, and civic groups, and supplemented the income of the railroads.

The change in tone from the twenties into the thirties was not dramatic. Albany's first radio station, WPC, began broadcasting in 1934. That same year, the city dedicated the Christmas lights to Franklin Delano Roosevelt for his efforts to deal with the Depression. While there were years of struggle ahead, his "Bank Holiday" had deterred scrambling depositors long enough so the banks could reopen with some degree of public confidence.

Locals were becoming familiar with the "alphabet soup" of agencies, especially the Agricultural Adjustment Administration (AAA). It sought to stabilize farm prices, promote conservation, and reclaim eroded land. Enormous gullies had cut into the south and its streams and rivers had churned red for generations with the runoff from north Georgia's farmlands. There were 307 Relief Districts in the country and southwest and south-central Georgia made up District 8—an enormous area including 34 of the state's larger counties.

The New Deal was the first real encounter between southwest Georgians and a powerful federal agency since the Freedmen's Bureau left at the end of Reconstruction. Many whites watched with caution. In the state as a whole, there was something of a class split as the poor found more to be hopeful about in New Deal measures. Social Security, wage and hour laws, new bridges, forest reclamation projects, dams, and the development of the Smoky Mountain National Forest left Georgians divided over whether it was better to avoid federal regulation than to become dependent on federal subsidies, even if the subsidies came from their own taxes.

Enthusiasm for FDR was apparently sufficient for the city commission to change the name of North Avenue to Roosevelt. Increasing community improvement was a significant byproduct of the public works projects of the New Deal. Parks and public facilities throughout the nation had their beginnings in this period, inspired by or paid for by federal programs. Chehaw Park, established in 1937, was one of Albany's achievements growing out of this movement.

Conceived as great public works to foster employment and get the economy moving again, the New Deal floundered briefly during the recession of 1937. Then, inexorably, the effort turned toward rearmament as U.S. relations with Japan deteriorated and our World War I allies found themselves desperate for our manufacturing capabilities while standing up to Hitler and Mussolini. FDR's policy of neutrality—like Wilson's before him—gradually eroded as American sympathies hardened after the Nazi invasion of Poland in September 1939.

But there were still good times in Albany at the twilight of the interwar years. The city celebrated its

Albany's fire department won a number of awards in the 1930s and 1940s under the leadership of Chief Dennis William "Bill" Brosnan (far left), one of the most respected fire-fighters in the country. Following the Tornado of 1940, it fell to Brosnan to head search, rescue and recovery efforts and to condemn property for demolition.

centennial year in the midst of the Depression. Nelson Tift's granddaughter was queen of the celebration held at Hugh Mills Memorial Stadium at Albany High. The program was designed by architect Edward Vason Jones, son of one of Albany's oldest families. A special 140-page edition of the *Herald* retold the story of Albany's founding. A pageant portrayed the city's history, institutions, and commerce.

Reading of this event today, one understands the nostalgia our fathers and grandfathers felt for the era before the war. For all the challenges overcome, who could have imagined what lay ahead in the next century?

The first bookmobile was something of a sensation in 1939. Another stir was created when the *Herald* in November carried news about the crew and cast of a Hollywood movie who had arrived here. Filming of "The Biscuit Eater" in Dougherty County drew local and state celebrities to meet the stars. Governor E.D. Rivers came down to gawk at the stars and camera crews. A traditional boy-meets-dog story, like "Good-bye My Lady" filmed here after the war, "The Biscuit Eater" drew its inspiration from the virtues of a simpler life, and gave notice to the rest of the country that southwest Georgia was the "Bird Dog Capital of the World." Both films made their premieres at the Albany Theater, built by the Sam Farkas Estate in 1927. (Farkas was a Hungarian Jew who had made a fortune in mules before the advent of tractors.)

The only local event to overshadow the war in

Europe was the tornado that struck Albany on February 10, 1940. It gave Albanians a sample of what London must have been suffering in the "Blitz." Fortunately for some, the tornado struck from the southwest before dawn. Like victims of other tornadoes, locals recalled the approaching storm sounding like a thousand freight trains. Witnesses guessed that the winds reached five hundred miles an hour as it leveled homes and crushed modern brick buildings in its course. Automobiles were hurled into the air, trees twisted into splinters.

18 people were dead or dying when the winds, after ripping the heavy tile roof off the train station, crossed the Flint. Destruction in the downtown district was heaviest east of North Washington and north of Pine. The A&P store was demolished and photographs show walls ripped down, but canned goods ironically still sitting undisturbed on the shelves. At the local Ford dealership, Haley Motors, 387 windows were shattered. The Gordon Hotel needed $35,000 in repairs.

National Guard units were mobilized to deter looters. Dazed and amazed people walked the downtown most of the day, looking in disbelief at what had happened. Property damage was estimated at between five and ten million dollars, a great deal for a small city to absorb.

By the following year, many businesses had been rebuilt or repaired. But even today, the damage wrought by the tornado can still be traced in vacant lots, patched buildings, and newer small buildings that never quite filled in the path of destruction. The railroad (Central of Georgia) immediately began repairs on the train station, re-roofing it with drab asbestos shingles, covering over where the two dormers had once broken the horizontal lines of the building. The porte cocheres were rebuilt from the heavy timbers that survived, but are today only half their original depth. Most of those killed were in frame houses southwest of downtown, a section mostly African American. One worker in the railyard was reportedly decapitated by a piece of flying tin roofing.

Before the Second World War, Albany was a small city by most standards. Its population only numbered about 25,000 in 1940. The war would bring many changes, including the migration of people to the town from many different places. They came to find wartime work at Turner Army Air Force Base and with the training program known as the Arnold Scheme for British and French Air Cadets to be done by civilians at Darr Aero Tech, Inc. Darr Aero Tech was located on the site of the municipal airport, while Miller Brewing occupies the expanse that was once Turner Field.

Darr Aero Tech was named for its owner H.S. Darr, who had joined the Army Air Corps during World War I. After his training as a pilot he became an instructor. Employed by the Curtis Company until 1932, he joined American Airlines in 1932. He later rented Curtis Field in Chicago as a commercial venture. In 1939, under the Arnold Scheme, he was awarded a contract to train "Flying Cadets," and established training bases in Albany and Augusta in Georgia, Lakeland in Florida, and Ponce City in Oklahoma.

The Arnold Scheme was named for Army Air Force commander Major General Henry H. "Hap" Arnold. In the months before the U.S. entered the war following the Japanese attack on Pearl Harbor, Arnold went to London to offer one-third of US pilot training facilities for the training of British pilots—hopefully about four thousand. To stay within the neutrality laws, civilian pilots at first conducted the training at facilities located at Arcadia and Lakeland in Florida, Albany and Americus in Georgia, Camden in South Carolina, and Tuscaloosa in Alabama. Darr Aero Tech, Inc. was the entity created to train pilots in Albany.

Albany families got to know these young men. Often they attended one of the downtown churches in

Cadets Pritchard, Tennant and Payne reading the Sunday papers outside Hut 3011 at Turner Field in early 1942. Albany was a hub of combat air training for US and Allied pilots during World War II.

response to invitations to services, but also to meet the girls in town. Many were welcomed into the homes of Albanians to share their Sunday dinners, listen to the radio or socialize with other young people. They were immensely popular and the bond has remained strong between those who trained here and those who became their wartime families.

The *Herald's* feature "Circling Turner Field" kept up with what was going on at the airfield. Many civilian employees came to Albany to take jobs at the military base. There was a terrific housing shortage during the war and many locals made extra money by renting out their guest room or adding an apartment over the garage. Housing continued to be in short supply until well after the war ended.

In a recent chance encounter, a veteran American pilot who trained in Albany recalled that the American boys sometimes referred to the Flint River as "Frenchman's Creek," because several French cadets became foolhardy and crashed in the water. In the end, the Arnold Plan trained more than four thousand British fliers, and many who "washed out" trained elsewhere and became navigators, bombardiers, wireless operators, and gunners. Some had later opportunities to complete their pilot training.

The heroic air defense of Britain by these young men in World War II defines the meaning of valor. We are lucky they were here with us for a season. RAF Memorial in Crown Hill Cemetery recalls the young air

First POW in World War II

*L*t. Col. Edwin M. Clements USMC (retired), who has lived in Albany for forty three years, attended Yengching University in northern China, where he became an accomplished linguist. Before World War II, he was stationed at Peking (Beijing) where he was assigned to work as our diplomatic and military courier. He served for a time as General Douglas MacArthur's interpreter. Later he became the first Comptroller at the Marine Corps Logistics Base, eventually retiring here in 1960. The following incident occurred prior to the Japanese attack on Pearl Harbor in December of 1941.

When the Germans invaded Poland (September 1939), and England and France went to war, I was down in Qinhuangdao and the Japanese (who had invaded China earlier) captured me there and held me for 31 days. And they moved me to a different location in China every night— they wouldn't move me in the daytime. Every night. I was in a freight car all that time, and they wouldn't let me get out. They wouldn't let me speak to anyone. I'd try to speak to them in Chinese and Russian and anything else, and nobody would do anything. If I started to get out of that freight car, they'd run at me with fixed bayonets, and those things don't snap.

....they never touched me during the whole thirty-one days. And on the thirty-first day—or thirty first night—they pulled me into the station in Peking and left and didn't say anything to anybody, or to me either.

When I woke up the next morning, I saw where I was, because I had been in the station so many times that I knew it by heart. I called my boss over there... who was a major, Leonard Earl Ray, and I told him where I was... I had thirty-one days of beard and was in a mess. I hadn't been able to take a bath because they wouldn't let me out of that car. And I didn't have enough water to take a bath or shave. I only had five gallons for that whole time.

Interview conducted by Christopher Fullerton for the Thronateeska Heritage Center Collection in 1998.

Over the years, many former British cadets would come back to Albany, especially from May to October 1991, when the fiftieth anniversary was observed. Their numbers have declined in recent years, but a stalwart group of locals** have kept alive the personal friendships and encouraged the pilgrimages to Albany that now span almost sixty years.

Two graduates of Madison High, a black school, won distinction in the war as fliers. Lt. William "Bill" Shepperd Hunter, one of the Tuskegee Airmen, flew seventy-four missions as a member of the 332nd Fighter Group. His school mate, Lt. Richard W. Hall, was awarded the Air Medal for service in the war and later served as an instructor at Tuskegee Army Air Field. This is of some note because in World War I black American pilots had flown British and French planes, only to be assigned ground duty after they joined American units when the U.S. entered the war.

Tragedy struck Albany in the very first attack on American forces in World War II. The *Herald* on December 8 announced that Walter B. Manning of Second Avenue and William Arthur Oxford of nearby Dawson were killed aboard the USS OKLAHOMA when Japanese air forces launched a surprise attack on U.S. military forces at Pearl Harbor. Albanians were fired by the same patriotic passion as other Americans and rushed to buy war bonds, to enlist for military service, or to enroll for home defense.

There were mixed signals in the *Herald*: announcements of blackout procedures (in case of an air raid one was to keep cool, stay home, lie down) were followed closely by an announcement that the seasonal Christmas lights would be "the brightest ever."

In November of 1941, the Safety Cab Company, in the face of a shortage of male cab drivers due to the draft and wartime employment conditions, advertised for women drivers and set off a public debate. One hundred and thirty seven women applied for the four positions, suggesting that there were many women who could not find employment even as the economy was moving to a wartime footing. When customers questioned the capabilities of women drivers, the manager expressed his belief that women could be "as competent as men." He added that women would not be expected to accept calls from "restricted areas."

In its ads, the "Black Cat" on the Leesburg Highway described itself as "Albany's favorite eating place." It retains an air of illicit mystery about it in locals' memories. Its ads said it was "open all night for

cadets who trained here. The training of seven men was cut short by deadly crashes.* Five recipients of the Victoria Cross (VC) were trained in Arnold schools. One of these, Flying Officer Cyril Joe Barton, received part of his training at Darr Aero Tech. Air Commodore (Ret.) Jack Frost also received Great Britain's highest military honor. He trained at Turner Field.

*Lieutenants Thomas Mosley (1919-1942), Robert Seymor Wilson (1921-1941), D'Arcy Harry Michael Wilson (1922-1941), Jack Hartley (1917-1941), Eric Nepean George Newberry (1921-1941), Dennis Hope (1923-1942) and Edward Stanley Headington (1921-1941) were killed during training and are buried at Crown Hill Cemetery.

**This group has included Robert "Bob" M. Drake, C. B. Pritchett Jr., John Sperry, John M. Sherman, Lamar Clifton, Harold Harden , (Mrs.) Bea Phillips, Whitfield Gunnels Jr., and others.

First Lieutenant William Sheppard Hunter of Albany (far right) was one of the Tuskegee Airmen during World War II. A fighter pilot, he flew 74 missions over enemy territory and was a flight instructor at the Tuskegee Army Air Field after returning home. US Army Air Corps photo from Aaron Brown, The Negro in Albany *(Privately printed, 1945). Photo courtesy of James Griffin.*

an evening of fun." On the Philema Road was "Lakeworth," offering bowling, dining, and dancing, typical roadhouse fare for the era. Just days before Pearl Harbor, Willie Mosconi was giving a pool shooting exhibition at the "Rialto," advertised as "Albany's Finest Billiard Parlor," located at 224 Pine.

The war years were exciting for many and there were the inevitable dislocations in the daily routine. A familiar family name could be found over the mayor's office. W.B. Haley served as mayor from 1939 until 1947. While many Albanians remember the rationing of gasoline, tires, and some foodstuffs, few recall well enough to complain about it at this late date. Many, instead, recall the war years with nostalgia because they felt a sense of unity and purpose that would be more elusive in the years ahead. They were the first generation to grow up hearing history being made over the radio. And the first in which popular music and films defined their generation. ❧

The Royal Air Force Memorial at Crownhill Cemetery was placed there in 1991. Near it lie the remains of RAF cadets killed in training at Turner Field and Darr Aero Tech and buried far from home in "some corner of a foreign field that is forever England."

CHAPTER IV

AFTER THE WAR

The End and Beginning of Eras 1945–1968

Nothing quite symbolizes teenage life in the post-World War II era like the drive-in restaurant. The Arctic Bear was an institution familiar to most young Albanians in the 1950s. Eating a hamburger in the car with one's date was— well, a date. Note the popularity of the '49-'50 Fords. They were powered by V-8 engines, an important status symbol among young men.

As the wars in Europe and the Pacific wound down, Albany entered an era of unprecedented social change and prosperity. This new generation, "tested in war" as President Kennedy would later characterize it, would see the emergence of African American aspirations, long deferred or denied. Shared wartime experiences and the Roosevelt administration's integration of the military gave wings to black hopes of gaining equality. When the tide of prosperity in the fifties failed to raise their dream-laden ship, black frustration welled up and shook the foundations of the nation, and of Albany.

In some ways, the most remarkable Albanians of the postwar era were Alice Coachman (later Davis), a black female athlete, and James H. Gray Sr., white male publisher and entrepreneur. Coachman, a product of Deep South segregation, managed to become an Olympic high jumper. Gray, a New Englander like Nelson Tift, was publisher of the *Herald*, brought television to Albany, and advocated the diehard segregationist position shared by many powerful white Georgians. The war, heroism, athletic prowess, and old-fashioned business acumen scrambled the formula for success. The old absolutes of family, race, and tradition were losing their hold.

For white families, there was a sameness about the structures of family and society. Successful careers often sprang from connections with businesses that had been important before the war: banking, law, real estate, and Coca-Cola. The wealthy and socially prominent were likely to be members of St. Paul's Episcopal or First Methodist. Before the war, they had attended the Citadel, Mercer, or the University of Georgia, although there were a handful who pursued more highly technical studies at Georgia Tech. A saying grew up that Mercer was for those too poor to go to Emory and too proud to go to Georgia.

Some were descendants of old plantation families, or married those who were. Fortunate marriages sometimes provided capital for ambitious young men. A stream of Coca-Cola connections ran through the prominent families of the forties and fifties. At the highest levels, there were the inevitable elections to bank or railroad boards. This pattern can hardly be ascribed to Albany alone; it characterized many Deep South towns of any size.

For married women, the way to social prominence was through a fortunate marriage and the opportunities afforded by leisure for service in cultural, patriotic, or religious organizations. The arts, music, the Daughters of the American Revolution, the United Daughters of the Confederacy, the Colonial Dames, garden clubs, and women-of-the-church organizations were all-white enclaves, but also opportunities for expressing a rising sense of self and service. Further down the social hierarchy, women expanded upon the secretarial-telephone operator-school teacher model as new opportunities appeared in traditional male professions and occupations. Before the divorce rate exploded in the 1960s, individual successes could hardly be counted as victory for women's equality. But the war had loosed the constraints of sex, family, and race. The decade was what the thirties might have been without the Depression.

Parallel patterns could be found in the black community, except that men found the church increasingly a friend to their aspirations as men and as blacks. It would be the churches around which the civil rights movement in Albany, as elsewhere, would swirl. There were also educators, both in the public schools and Albany State College, who could counter the argument that blacks were unfit for full participation in political life because they were uneducated. Civic Clubs were similar in focus and organization, and one could find some of the wealthiest black businessmen in the Criterion Club. Soon, medicine, dentistry, and the law would afford unprecedented opportunities, first within the black community and later outside of it. Social prominence for black women was to be found in the benevolent and religious organizations that mirrored those across the color line. There was much about the two societies that was all but identical.

Freed at last from decades of grim farming and slow development, the South after the war found that prosperity brought unimagined challenges. Black and white, male and female, child and adult, most people were about to witness a season of incredible change. There would be little time to savor the memories—the sad and the sweet—of the war years. It may be worth postulating that the Second World War did more to change the South than the Civil War.

Wars often mark the arrival of new eras. For almost two decades, the economic impact of the war shaped Albany's destiny. In the closing months of the war 4,000 citizens turned out to celebrate the 38th anniversary of the founding of the Aviation Branch of the U.S. Army. "A holiday spirit prevailed in Albany today," said the *Herald*, "Virtually all places of business were closed for the day-long program at Turner (Air Field)." A "two-hour flying exhibition of Billy Mitchell bombers and a B-29 flyover thrilled watchers," still enthusiastically patriotic despite the wartime sacrifices. From the earliest days of pilot training, the area had a strong connection with the military and with the federal government.

Earlier in the year, Lowell Thomas, the author and newscaster, came to Albany to address a graduating class of pilots. His son was an instructor at the Turner advanced school for pilots. His visit made the front

An Armed Forces Day parade in 1953. Broad Street is lined with palm trees planted before WWI. Thronateeska Heritage Center Collection.

page. So did Governor Ellis Arnold's visit in April. He was stumping for the new constitution which was to be voted on in the fall.

For the most part, though, it was the world news that captured locals' attention. Defeated Germany's future looked grim, but the immense new power of the Soviet Union made the Allies slow to give up on Germany as a future democratic power. Even as the Nazi War Crimes Tribunal got under way, the wartime cooperation between the U.S. and the Soviet Union began to disintegrate. The Cold War ahead would guarantee Albany's continuing value as a military installation. Prosperity would follow in the wake of the greatest peacetime military build up in U.S. history.

Notwithstanding the preoccupation with the news from Europe and the Far East, where the war continued, there were exciting rumblings that the production of passenger cars, suspended for the duration of the war, might soon be starting up again. The pent-up buying power of the war years was about to explode. So was the population. Shortly, the "war babies," as they were then called, would outstrip the county's ability to educate them. Crowded schools were about to become the norm. So was the housing shortage. A building boom, postwar inflation, and the GI Bill, providing

money for discharged soldiers to enroll in college, all affected Albany.

On August 6, 1945, an ominous headline broke in the *Herald*: President Truman announced the destruction of the Japanese city of Hiroshima by an atomic bomb. On the 12th, a false rumor swept through town that the Japanese had surrendered. Then on the 15th, the city went wild with excitement as the genuine peace announcement came with "hoops, auto horns, prayers, and tears." Substituting toilet paper for confetti, roomers at the Hotel Gordon showered the street below.

A prophetic speculation in the *Herald* claimed that wartime restrictions on athletics were about to be lifted and that Japan's surrender was "expected to usher in a Golden Age of U.S. athletics." Gas coupons were shredded and littered gas station lots as drivers filled up their tanks. The war was really over. An editorial in the *Herald* of August 6 was predictably optimistic about the future:

"Albany will take up where she laid down nearly four years ago and continue to lead the cities of Georgia in the march of progress. She will establish new industry, some already being built. Present industry will be enlarged. Our local governments are prepar-

Sedge, briars, pointing dogs, quail and shotguns—the right ingredients for a day afield. Southwest Georgia is the quail capital of the world.

ing to make material contributions. Many new homes will be built. Its geographic position gives it great advantage, but the quality of its citizenship is its greatest asset."

The writer proved accurate in his prediction about housing, at least white housing. During the following years, there was a building boom in Albany. In July, city building permits reached their highest mark ever. Housing, schools, and businesses led the way. Schools would continue to be overcrowded for several years as wartime babies came of school age. Public housing financed by federal funds began to appear as the government sought to cure the problem of substandard housing for the poor by building the "projects," large apartment-style buildings that in some cases would themselves become little more than slums. Again, Albany's experience differed little from that of other cities.

In Albany, as in much of the South, the projects were for blacks. Built in black neighborhoods, they often replaced existing black housing. Reinforcing traditional patterns of segregation, they would give way to even more controversial housing initiatives that brought low-cost, single family or duplex houses into or near white neighborhoods. The prewar shift in the population continued and 1950 would be the first census in which whites were the majority.

Another indicator of change: in 1947 there were five hotels in downtown Albany. They would all be replaced by the newer "motels" or motor courts by

the end of the century.

The postwar years were filled with oddities. Early in 1947, Albany had its first flying saucer sighting. In July, A.T. Spires and his family reported seeing an unidentified flying saucer for about ten minutes in the early evening. Such sightings were a nationwide phenomena and experts were dismissing them as having been caused by weather balloons.

Whatever caused these, sightings have persisted to the end of the century and public fascination with the possibility of alien visitations continues to be a topic of popular television and motion pictures—now, just as in the late forties and early fifties. In fact, in 1957, when the Russians launched their earth satellite "Sputnik," everyone had a chance to marvel over the prospects of space travel. In the fall of that year, the satellite was clearly visible in the evening skies over Georgia. Of course, this technological leap reawakened fears of Soviet missile capabilities, a fear that John Kennedy would exploit as the "missile gap" in his presidential campaign of 1960.

The "Red Menace," as the spread of international communism was called then, would continue to be a major concern throughout the lifetimes of Americans born before and during the Second World War. To deal with the threat of Soviet military weaponry, the United States established the Strategic Air Command made up of huge B-52 jet-powered bombers capable of delivering nuclear bombs to other continents. Theoretically, some of these planes were always airborne in case of a surprise Soviet attack. Such planes were based here at Turner Air Force Base. They were complemented by a Nike missile system.

Spy flights by U-2 planes helped monitor Soviet missile capabilities. It is reported that Francis Gary Powers, an Air Force pilot stationed in Albany and married to an Albany girl, was recruited by CIA agents staying at the New Albany Hotel. Powers was later shot down over the Soviet Union, an event that set Soviet-American relations on edge for several months.

Fear of Communism poisoned many relationships. The South, traditionally hostile toward organized labor, was willing to believe that walkouts and strikes were the work of communists and their sympathizers. In October 1948, Albany workers at the Clark Thread Company, given an opportunity to vote to establish a union shop, rejected it 534 to 200. For the next 50 years, such anti-labor sentiments were cited as an inducement for industries to locate to the South. Indeed, the entire nation would become far less sympathetic to labor organizations in the 1950s because some unions had connections with organized crime.

Another "threat" to southern white traditions was the rising expectations of the formerly unseen, unheard, and underrepresented black population. The white population was wondering what the "payoff" would be for the blacks who had served their country so well in the war. Cautious public acknowledgment of individual blacks came in the "tokenism" of the period.

Alice Coachman was one of those who won such recognition. Born in Albany in 1921, she was the third child in a family of six. A fleet-footed track star at Monroe High, she won early admission to Tuskegee Institute for her "natural running powers." In 1939, Coachman won a national title in the high jump. She was an ASU star throughout the 1940s in the broad and high jumps, as well as the 50 and 100 meter dashes.

The peak of Coachman's career came in 1948 when she won the gold medal for the high jump at the London Olympic Games. Albany State celebrated with a special program for Coachman at the college. Popular mayor J.W. "Taxi" Smith sent his congratulations, which appeared in the program for the event. In the style of the day, he praised Coachman as a "credit to her race." Coachman was also honored at a convocation in the Municipal Auditorium attended not only by blacks but by whites as well. It was a tentative but positive beginning.

Southwest Georgia preferred the regular Democratic Party presidential candidate in 1948, even though incumbent Truman came close to losing the election because the party was divided. Southern Rights advocates, irritated by Truman's internationalism and steamed over the Marshall Plan (not to mention Truman's continuing sympathy for black civil rights), held their own convention and nominated South Carolina's Senator Strom Thurmond on the "Dixiecrat Ticket." Southern congressmen continued to harangue their northern compatriots, warning them not to outlaw the poll tax or job discrimination. It turned out that 1948's conflicts were the tip of iceberg of race politics.

If Albany's Democrats were wary of the national party, they were nonetheless delighted when party politics in Washington tossed a big plum to the area's economy. In January of 1951, it was confirmed in an announcement by U.S. Senator Carl Vinson that a "huge Marine Depot was to be built in the community" at an initial cost of $20,000. Commissioned in 1952, the "Marine Corps Depot of Supplies" would become the "Marine Corp Logistics Base, Albany" in 1954. Eventually, inventory and control functions would be shifted here from Pennsylvania, making the base a critical link in our national defense system.

Whatever rancor existed between the sectional wings of the party, it was obvious that Congress' seniority system had enabled Vinson, as head of the Armed Services Committee, to create yet another military installation in the state.

Although General Eisenhower was elected to the presidency in the fall, the Democrats would continue to control Congress throughout the decade and the South would be checkered with military bases. Macon, Augusta, Columbus, and Albany, as well as other cities in the state, were all helped by Representative Vinson in this way.

Many of our generation who grew up in Georgia in the 1950s were little concerned about politics. Instead, we recall the fear our parents had for us when it came to getting out in large groups or going swimming because of an epidemic of poliomyelitis or "polio." Children were particularly susceptible to the disease and it seemed that every school class had at least one victim. We all knew someone stricken by the crippling disease.

Dougherty County's 20 cases in 1951 were the highest of any county in the state. Dr. Jonas Saulk's perfection of the vaccine for polio in 1954 saved many and left many for whom there was no cure. But slowly, the "Iron Lung," a huge apparatus used by polio victims to breath, was seen less and less in the news, and the grimacing faces of children receiving their "shots" became common fare in the weekly news and photo magazines.

President Franklin Roosevelt was crippled by polio and used the waters at Warm Springs to try to restore strength to his weakened legs. Thus, many Georgians had a particular empathy with polio victims. Mrs.

Mildred Nix Huie worked to create the Albany Crippled Children's Clinic. The commercial manager for WALB-TV, she was also active in the Tuberculosis Association. A graduate of Shorter College in Rome, she had been born in Augusta. A member of the American Association of University Women and of the local school board, she was one of the early proponents of a junior college here.*

In 1954, there was a move to have Albany State College changed into a trade school.** Local leaders, black and white, succeeded in defeating this, but the college was losing enrollment and there was some dissatisfaction with President Aaron Brown. By merely pointing out the squalor and lack of economic progress in a 1945 book, *The Negro in Albany*, Dr. Brown had upset many conservatives by implying that the lives of blacks could and should be better. He was not rehired for the 1955 academic year, but went on to a distinguished academic career elsewhere.

In the fifties, rapid change occurred alongside the ways of the past. A January 1951 issue of the *Herald* featured an ad for the annual Fat Cattle Show alongside an ad for the new 1951 Kaiser automobile. One of a handful of postwar challenges to the "Big Three" automakers, Kaiser combined technical innovations with stylish modern lines. Sumner Motor Company on Front Street advertised the Kaiser as the "Only Car with Anatomic Design." In the record-sales years of the fifties, even outdated Packard Motor Company held out against the behemoths of Detroit. But like the Tucker (one of which sat in a showroom of an Albany machine shop for years), these cars could not bring the necessary capital to bear continuously on the two-year cycle of redesign that came to be expected by the American buying public. "New, longer, lower, more powerful" became the mantra of Detroit and Dearborn.

In the spring of 1954, television came to Albany when James Gray's WALB-TV began broadcasting. In an ironic twist, sound was lost during the first day's broadcast. But no matter. Ads for TV sets dotted the newspapers for the first time. Those who remember TV in those days recall the white blur that passed for reception and the hazy images on screen that we were assured were people. Even test patterns were a novelty for a while. Television antennas sprouted on the tops of houses everywhere, a new status symbol for those "rich" enough to own one. Admissions to the hospital recorded a new casualty in the war of household injuries: the do-it-yourself TV antenna installer.

Early programming on WALB consisted mainly of old movies, cartoons, and locally produced kiddie shows. Grady Shadburn starred in the series "Ringo and the Lazy-A Ranch" and later "The Captain Mercury Show." Captain Mercury was inexplicably from the planet Zeus. Shortly, soap operas in the early afternoon and the ubiquitous variety shows would flood Albany's living rooms. CBS President David H. Cogan was quoted in the *Herald* as saying that TV would "bring a new strength to home and family bonds." Furniture and houses would soon be designed around the TV set and our language would be sprinkled with TV references such as "frozen TV dinners," "TV trays," "rabbit ears" (two-armed indoor antennas), "antenna rotors" (to adjust the antenna with an electric motor), and "Howdy Doody" (a popular children's program also watched by many adults).

Madison Avenue had a new medium beaming into practically every home. Along with its message would come a new tradition: dinner spent watching the evening news. And the news would bring the conflicts of the civil rights and antiwar movements into our homes.

Despite the signs of change that were everywhere in the fifties and the slow progress of black civil rights, these years were the best of times for some. For business, especially military-based industries and those tied to automobile manufacturers, it was a golden age. New industries like advertising, chain groceries, ultramodern service stations, highway construction firms, contractors, and plastic manufacturers all flourished.

Roads radiating out of Albany were improved. Slappey Drive was paved in the early fifties. New stores were being built away from the traditional center of town. They began to dot the edges of Slappey, Dawson, and the streets that connected Albany to the Marine Depot and Turner Field. New businesses were moving with the expanding suburbs. Road and traffic changes were undermining downtown's control of retail markets. In April 1956, a Spring Arts Festival commemorated the 50th anniversary of the Albany Carnegie Library. It featured ballet, art, and plays—the "finer things" in life. It was the first of many activities aimed at keeping people coming downtown.

Prosperous, segregated, and progressive, white Albany was proud of its past and seemed to feel little anxiety about the future. A city of 50,000 when John F. Kennedy was elected President (1960), Albany was 40 percent black and totally segregated.

For our generation, this is about the point of separation between clear and detailed memories, which are more recent, and those imperfect and somewhat overheated memories of our growing up. The racial upheavals of the

---

* Mrs. Huie "retired" to St. Simons Island where she spent her time painting, managing her gallery, The Left Bank, and writing histories of the coastal plantations. Albany Junior College opened in 1965.
** Albany Technical Institute would be established in 1961.

GENE AUTRY'S SIDEKICK

*M*ilitary assignments have brought remarkable and interesting people to Albany over the years. Cindy Lou Dahl was both. She was an actress, TV personality and a cowgirl with incredible skills. For four years in the 1950s, she hosted the Melody Ranch Show as the "Gal Foreman" of Gene Autry's "spread." Along with Roy Rogers, Autry was the singing and shooting matinee idol of millions of children and not a few adults and Melody Ranch was broadcast daily in many parts of the country.

Cindy was no passive partner. An accomplished horse woman, she competed in barrel and quarter racing. She was also billed as the "Fastest Gal-Gunfighter" and could draw and fire her six-shooter in three-tenths of a second. Cindy used the spotlight her talents afforded her to work with U.S. Attorney General Herbert Brownell to fight juvenile delinquency in the Washington, D.C. area. Cindy appeared on the Dave Garroway Show, Dragnet, and with Roy Rogers and Dale Evans (Roy's on- and off-screen wife).

Cindy was married to an Air Force officer whose career took them to Europe and throughout the United States. While in Washington, D.C. in the sixties, she worked as a TV weather reporter and served as Public Relations Director of the Republican Governors' Conference. After she and her husband came to Albany, Cindy worked in radio and did promotional work for worthy causes. Her celebrity status also made her a regular in local parades. Cindy died in 1994 and is buried at Crown Hill Cemetery.

early sixties, the assassination of the President and the beginning of the war in Southeast Asia would define our national life for decades to come. For those of us in college, these seemed like distant events, but ones about which we were expected to have ideas and opinions.

Seemingly timeless social conventions were on the verge of collapse as Albanians entered the 1960s. In 1954, the U.S. Supreme Court in Brown *v.* the Board of Education of Topeka reversed its 60-year stance on the principle of "separate but equal" public education. In November 1961, new Interstate Commerce Commission guidelines took effect requiring the desegregation of all trains, buses, airplanes, and terminal facilities engaged in interstate commerce.

Later that month, a coalition of black civic organizations was created, known as the Albany Movement. After five black college students were arrested for a "sit-in" at the Trailways Bus Station lunch counter, this group called the first of several mass meetings at Mt. Zion Baptist Church. Out on bail, the students told of their experiences in jail and the movement gained energy from the Freedom Singers. When the students were tried on the 27th, there were mass marches that expectedly drew the condemnation of the *Herald* and much of the white establishment.

Then on December 10, nine Freedom Riders arrived to test the segregated train station. An architectural embodiment of segregation, the station had two waiting rooms—one white, one black—dating from the pre-World War I era when "separate but equal" was acceptable to the Supreme Court and mandated by state law. The riders were arrested in the street after they left the station. Albany Police Chief Laurie Pritchett, a clever and careful tactician, waited until they were off federally regulated property and on a local public street, Roosevelt Avenue.

When the Freedom Riders' trial began, over 400 were arrested in two days of demonstrations. Albany Movement President William Anderson invited the Reverend Martin Luther King Jr. to Albany to keep the pressure on local officials to negotiate with black leaders. On December 15, King spoke to overflow crowds at Shiloh and Mt. Zion Baptist Churches. The next day, King and 264 demonstrators were arrested when they marched to City Hall.

While the methods followed in the protests were similar to those used in other famous confrontations, Chief Pritchett avoided overcrowding the city jail by shipping those arrested to jails in neighboring towns. And he had diligently coached his men not to initiate violence or provoke the demonstrators.

Bob's Candies, a white-owned business, canceled its interracial Christmas Party until a genuine start could be made at meeting the concerns of its black employees. Christmas in Albany was a time of anger and frustration. King had been released from jail with an oral commitment by city leaders to hear the concerns of the Albany Movement. When the city showed itself unwilling to negotiate, blacks boycotted the city transit system.

On February 27, King was convicted of disorderly conduct and failing to obtain a permit to march. Sentencing was delayed. Behind the scenes, at least some Albanians were ready to see the matter dealt with so as not to bring discredit to the community. Inquiries by President Kennedy (a friend of *Herald* editor James Gray) and New York's Governor Nelson Rockefeller escalated national press coverage.

When King returned to Albany for sentencing on July 13, he was given a choice of a fine of $178 or 45 days in jail. King chose jail, but his fine was delivered by his white attorney, B.C. Gardner. This was apparently orchestrated by white community leaders who wanted King out of town. On the 17th, King spoke at Mt. Zion, encouraging protesters with the prediction that their efforts would "turn Albany upside down." Barred from further marches by a Federal court order, King left Albany.

Many have debated whether King's effort in Albany was a success or failure and what contributions the Albany Movement made to the national civil rights movement. City officials claimed they had broken the back of the movement. King asserted that segregation was on its deathbed in Albany. Two things are clear. There was an indigenous civil rights movement in Albany before King; and King's visit galvanized local blacks' determination for social justice. It also seems a reasonable conclusion that King's visit hardened the determination of opponents of the movement in Albany.

These were the times of sowing. There were no firehoses, no attack dogs to quell demonstrators. While some of those arrested faced humiliating circumstances and discomfort, they did so with courage. And they inspired some whites to rethink old ways. Federal court edicts drove the process afterward. In 1964, the Dougherty County School System was desegregated.

Afterward, Albany would be integrated racially in most public ways. School politics and "white flight" to the suburbs combined with other factors to cause the decline of the inner city and the development of new "shopping centers." An expanding system of roads, including a new four-lane bypass, new housing subdivisions, new industry and growing employment opportunities would characterize most of the following three decades, although there were to be setbacks along the way.

Almost as a "sign" of the passing of the old guard

Chief Laurie Pritchett (wearing tie) talks with black demonstrators during the trial of the Reverend Martin Luther King, Jr. in 1962. A.C. Searles, newspaperman, stands in the center background. Photo Courtesy of Albany Police Department.

in Albany, the editor emeritus of the *Herald*, Henry MacIntosh, died on July 20, 1965. It was MacIntosh who sold the *Herald* to James Gray. In his generation, newspapermen guarded vigorously their role as defenders of the public, gadfly of government and generally maintaining good public morality. He was a character much beloved and a man knowledgeable about Albany's history, as few are today.

It may seem ironic, but the major political figure in Albany in the 1960s was undoubtedly James H. Gray. A Yankee from Massachusetts and a Dartmouth graduate, he had no trouble adapting the "rock ribbed" conservatism of New England to the defense of states' rights and segregation.

An airborne officer in World War II, he returned home and took a job in newspaper work. A gifted speaker and writer, Gray married well and became head of Gray Communications, parent corporation of WALB-TV and the *Albany Herald*. A determined businessman, Gray acquired other TV stations and built transportation and distribution companies as well. Five times president of the Chamber of Commerce, he received practically every honor that could be bestowed on an Albany businessman.

A newspaperman at heart, he was—like many newspaper editors before him—drawn into politics. His rise to prominence in the Democratic Party might have led him to the governor's mansion. Tied to the Talmadge political camp, he was the first non-native to head the Georgia Democratic Party. At the 1960 Los Angeles convention that nominated John F. Kennedy,

he delivered the southern minority report on the civil rights plank of the platform. His hard-nosed segregationist stand was typical of the lower South's stance at the time. His connections reached to high places. He hosted his friend, Senator John F. Kennedy, when Kennedy spoke at the "Woman of the Year" Banquet in 1957. But the governorship—or whatever political prize he may have sought—was not to be his.

In 1966, when incumbant Governor Vandiver had to drop out of the race because of a heart attack, Gray jumped into the fray, finishing only fourth behind Ellis Arnall, Lester Maddox, and Jimmy Carter. In 1974, Gray backed Maddox instead of eventual winner Albanian George Busbee. Future-governor Carter bounced Gray from his post as Democratic Party chief. Carter's political star was on the rise because his more liberal stance on integration fitted better with the new political realities.

After the late sixties, Georgia Democratic politics moderated somewhat. Gray went on to serve as the city's mayor for nearly a decade and a half, beginning in 1973. His local political reign was almost total, and he used this power to promote economic development, a superior medical facility, and downtown revitalization. His ways have been criticized by some and his successes discounted by others. His friends remained loyal. He controlled the newspaper, television, and the courthouse. His leadership was hard to resist, and his vision for Albany's future seems to have had no serious challengers. As his son Jimmy said in a *Herald* editorial after his father's death, "...he possessed that elusive aura of preordained accomplishment. . . "

Gray might have faired better in state politics if the county unit system had not been dismantled when he was nearing the height of his influence. This system of government had allowed the less populous rural counties to predominate over urban ones. It was finally ended following a court battle. From the 1960s on, the growing population of Atlanta would draw off most of the political power that had once rested in central and southwest Georgia. Rising political awareness and voter drives among blacks changed the way politics were played out in most of south Georgia.

Those crazy days of Georgia politics, when a Republican ("Bo" Callaway) got the most votes for Governor and the Legislature (mostly Democrats) elected Lester Maddox instead, are a reflection of how confusing Georgia politics can be. Increasingly, white Georgians became Republican in national politics and voted Democratic in state races. In 1964, Republican Senator Barry Goldwater garnered the Georgia electoral votes, even though he was running against a southerner, incumbant President Lyndon B. Johnson. It was not lost on southerners—black or white—that Democrat Johnson had pushed through the greatest change in voting rights and welfare in the country's history.

Still, many things remained more or less constant. There would be no crucial interstate connection for Albany. The steady growth of the metropolitan area continued. Churches would, for the most part, remain segregated. So would schools. Federally mandated integration, as James Gray had predicted, failed to insure integration of the public schools. Many became largely black. More affluent whites fled to new school districts, private academies, or even out of the county, maintaining that the mostly black schools were inferior. The lines became blurred between white segregationists and white parents fearful that their children's education would be undermined. Whatever the motive, the result was segregation. So, Albany experienced the anguish, conflict, and renewed segregation that tormented much of the nation from the late 1960s on.

Evidence of continuity as well as change was everywhere in the sixties. Many churches retained the families that had been in attendance for decades. Memories of World War II were still vivid. On Pearl Harbor Day in 1961, John Purvis recalled his memories of the Japanese attack while his destroyer the SHAW was in dry-dock. The military presence persisted. New manufacturing businesses had largely replaced farms as employers. Fewer than 800 individuals indicated they worked on farms in Dougherty County in the federal census of 1960.

Housing patterns remained somewhat the same,

except that historic properties began to disappear at an astonishing rate. They were victims of both progress and neglect. Later, efforts at downtown modernization altered the fabric of the inner city, as quaint old buildings gave way to modern ones, or worse became empty lots. Part of this resulted from population growth and sprawl. The metropolitan population was growing. It more than doubled between 1950 and 1970, from 44,000 to 97,000.

In Albany, Iris Court, one of the few remaining intown antebellum homes, was on the verge of destruction in 1965. Edward Vason Jones, an architect and neo-classicist, saved the house by convincing Charles Owen Smith Jr. to move it to Moultrie and return it to its former glory.

Jones became known nationally for his renovation of the U.S. State Department Diplomatic Reception Rooms between 1965 and 1980. Although Jones designed and restored a number of Georgia buildings, including the Shackleford House (1949-51) and the W.C. Holman Jr. home (1948), both in Albany, not even his influence could stem the destruction of historic buildings in Albany. His inspiration was to be found in the past, but Albany's fondness for the past succumbed to the temptations of progress and commerce in the decades after World War II.

Nearby Thomasville and Americus, cities that experienced no great growth after the war, retained much of their historic fabric and are now feeling the economic benefits of historic preservation movements. As executive director of Thronateeska in the 1970s, Eric Montgomery and others helped organize the preservation movement in Albany, but it died when he left to manage similar efforts in Thomasville and later Augusta. It would not be until 1996 that Albany would revive its historic preservation efforts, again under Thronateeska's leadership. By then, the task would be daunting.

Inflation was much talked about in the fifties, but did not really take off until the late sixties. In the early sixties, consumer prices were more like the 1940s than the 1980s. A nice Western Flyer bike sold for $39.88, a decent suit could still be had for 40 or 50 dollars, and T-bone steak was 99 cents a pound. Perhaps most importantly, television sets were roughly the price of a good console radio in the 1930s ($188). A used 1955 Ford—considered a classic even then—could be bought for $125, and a 1960 Ford Galaxy could be purchased for $1295. For under $17 a stylish young dresser could own a "suburban" coat. In 1961, a three-bedroom brick duplex rented for $60 a month and a large brick home on 5th Street was listed for $18,000. Savelle's offered a Keystone home movie camera for $159.

The Albany Civil Rights Memorial was dedicated November 20, 1993. The other marble tablets list the major events in the national and local civil rights movements.

Ray Charles, who was born in Albany, recorded two wildly successful hits in 1959. One was "What'd I Say," part of the fraternity dance rituals for the next decade. The other was "Georgia on My Mind," destined to become the new state song, and thankfully one to which most people would know the words.

On record players, teenagers and college students were listening and dancing to the music of the Shirelles ("Tonight's the Night," 1961) and the Supremes ("Stop! In the Name of Love,"1965) as the Motown Sound brought black music onto the pop charts. White sports coats were still appropriate at senior proms, as were long dresses. For less formal dress, young women wore "sack" dresses, made fashionable by the First Lady. Even the vigorous young president, his wife, and their entourage were doing the "Mashed Potato" and the "Twist."

Double-dating, souped-up "muscle cars" and the supercharged guitars of the Beach Boys were among the sources of teenage fun, excitement, and romance. Few who heard the wheezy harmonica and raspy voice of Bob Dylan ("Blowin' in the Wind," "With God on Our Side") could believe he would have much staying power. We would have been the last to predict that he would receive one of the Kennedy Center Honors 30 years later. And except for college students off at Emory or the University, few had heard of folk singer Joan Baez ("Just a Little Rain," "Hard is the Fortune of All Womankind").

And the war in Vietnam seemed distant except to the young men called to fight there. It seems the wild experimentation of the sixties never really caught on in Albany, where conservative values held sway and a general distrust of the federal government's encroaching power was paired with staunch patriotism. Like many young people, those in southwest Georgia undoubtedly took some refuge in the—at first—intellectually undemanding music of the Beatles, or caught the "Rock-a-Billy" wave, as rock and roll traditionalists tried to distance themselves from the acid rock and heavy metal sounds of the late sixties and early seventies.

The sixties were exciting, unnerving, and promising, all at once. For most of us at the time, the significance was lost in the demands of everyday life. Still, we can all recall where we were when the news came that our president had been murdered in Dallas on November 22, 1963. ?❧

CHAPTER V

IN OUR OWN TIMES

Challenges and Opportunities in a New City 1968–Present

The flood of 1994 was another reminder that in times of heavy rain, the Flint River could turn from blessing to curse. Albany State University was one segment of the community challenged by the river. Photo courtesy of the Army Corps of Engineers.

*I*t is difficult to say exactly what is and what is not history when it comes to writing about our own times. And our memories deceive us. We have lived most of the past thirty years in southwest Georgia, raising our children, practicing our professions, and taking in the life of the region. What defines our times are the media and electronic innovations that have finally knit the country into one community. International and national events are as near as the television or the car radio. By the 1970s, we were no longer tied to local news reports or network stations. Cable television had spawned a plethora of news channels and few households used outdoor antennas. We would watch the Gulf War (1991) live and in color, compliments of CNN reporters in Baghdad and circling communications satellites. Cheered by the prospect or not, we have found ourselves in the "global community."

The decades do stand out as arbitrary, but convenient, benchmarks of time. We remember the seventies as a time when we tried to forget the tumult of the sixties. As the war in Vietnam and the strife within the country subsided, music and clothing styles, for a season, took a strange turn as disco became an alternative to "heavy metal" and the outlandish dress of the "hippies" gave way to stacked heels, polyester leisure suits, and gaudy, flowered acetate shirts. Even normally conservative male dressers, like bankers and accountants, were sporting bell bottom trousers, wide collars, and ties so wide that two sewn together would make a bed cover.

We indulged ourselves in self-help books (*I'm O.K, You're O.K.* and *Your Erroneous Zones*, to mention two of a seemingly endless supply). Motion pictures such as the "Star Wars" trilogy provided unapologetic escapism.

Marines at the Logistics Base secure a tank for transport on a flatcar. Railroad access has been key to the continuance of the military base in Albany. MCLB photo.

By the 1970s, politics in Albany had taken a certain tone as C. B. King, successful attorney and outspoken civil rights leader, and James H. Gray Jr. held center stage. Their careers span a crucial era in the city's history. Although Gray's chance at the governor's office had passed in part because of his vehement stand on "states right," he continued to be the most eloquent spokesman for economic progress in our part of the world. King, of whom it was said that he was at one time the only black attorney practicing south of Atlanta, continued to be a vigorous civil rights advocate and social gadfly.

Gray owned the major newspaper, the TV station, and served as mayor as well. He was also a man with many admiring followers. Friends from that era remember his sound judgment, strong presence, and powerful intellect. His good writing and speaking abilities would have made him influential at any rate. His determination to see his adopted home prosper continued unabated until his death in 1986.

The Civic Center, completed in 1983, is a monument to Gray's determination to revitalize the city. And the demolition of buildings in Central Square in the mid-sixties was to have presaged the coming of a new downtown. Unfortunately, the economy in the 1970s and 1980s did not encourage rising expectations. Shaken by the effects of out-of-control gasoline prices, inflation, and unemployment, the economy of southwest Georgia took a tumble.

In making its report, a 1972 "Governmental Study Commission" defined the issues that would shape the city's political debates for the remainder of the century. The report criticized "the apparent apathy existing toward the exploitation of certain unique natural areas for individual and/or commercial development rather than for recreation or open space uses." This was an obvious reference to the river corridor. It also noted "the deterioration of older residential neighborhoods that surround the central core and the resultant negative effects upon human values and social conditions."

Preoccupied with racial and economic issues, it would be the 1990s before community leaders would grapple with these problems through such agencies as the Albany-Dougherty Inner City Authority, Albany Tomorrow Inc., and Historic Albany. Finally, the Commission cautioned that the population of the unincorporated metropolitan statistical area would explode in the years ahead, a prediction that came true in the form of extensive new housing and commercial development in adjacent Lee County.

There was hope, of course, that things would get better. In 1972, Proctor and Gamble started building a plant here. The Albany Mall, designed by Richard V. Richard, was opened in 1976. In 1980, the Miller

The flood of 1994 forced many people from their homes, especially along the creeks north of town and in the low-lying residential neighborhoods on the south side. The flood of 1998, although much less destructive, was a stern reminder that we live in the cradle of the river. The view of the flood from the air was spectacular.

Brewing plant was built on the site of the old Turner Air Force Base. The Miller-Albany marriage has proved a good one and Miller has contributed generously to civic and nonprofit agencies to improve the life of the city. In fact, most the newer industries in Albany, their corporate consciences sharpened by media revelations of the depth of need in the country, have followed the same helpful course.

If no interstate yet reached to Albany, at least there was the new bypass, enabling a driver to get from the James Rivers Motel on North Slappey to East Five Points in five minutes. Why this was thought necessary at the time we never fully understood, but it was also another reason not to go downtown, unless you were just passing through. And we all got a kick out of the new span over the Flint, a "Bridge to Nowhere" that predated the bypass. The emerging maze of one-way streets downtown suggests that the object was to get people through town as quickly as possible, an approach that did little for downtown businesses. One-way streets also seemed to contribute to the decline of inner-city neighborhoods, leaving many homes sitting alongside five o'clock freeways where the speed limits were, and are still routinely ignored.

Although well meaning, facelifts and beautification projects designed to keep shoppers coming to the downtown had little success. Indeed, false facades applied to the older buildings did little more than underscore the desperate situation. Mayor Gray's opening up of the central square in 1986 as the logical site for new inner-city development was incomplete when he died and efforts are still underway to piece together those elements that can make the downtown

vital again.

Albany, like so many cities across the nation, found that concern over crime, personal convenience, and the automobile all conspired to drive retail business out to the affluent suburbs. By the 1980s, the "Great Northwest" was sprouting "Category Killer" stores so large that smaller, same-category business concerns were drying up not only in Albany but in neighboring towns. Again, this phenomenon was not unique to Albany; it was a nationwide trend begun when Wal-Mart stores began to spread in the 1970s.

The national bicentennial occurred in 1976 and historical references abounded during the various celebrations. A little-known commemoration occurred in Albany, Texas. The town was named for Albany, Georgia by one of the Texas city's founders (W.R. Cruger, 1842-1882). Texas had incurred a debt in particular for the terrible tragedy that occurred when Mexican forces captured, then murdered, the "Georgia Battalion" at Goliad. Georgia had forgiven the offer of monetary payment for its help on condition that Texas erect a memorial to the fallen Georgians. After more than a century, the debt was honored and Texas built a monument in Albany. When it was dedicated, "Lady Bird" Johnson was among the dignitaries present, along with Georgia Governor George Busbee.

1976 also saw the city presented with a plaque commemorating the life of Wallingford Riegger (1885-1961). The son of a local lumber mill owner, Riegger had spent most of his life in New York as a composer. He was well known in music circles for his arrangements and interpretations of the works of the classical composers. Serious music has always had a small but

Looking from the north, the downtown is to the upper right, the Flint is to the left, and the railyard is in the foreground.

devoted following in Albany, as attested by the successes of the Albany Symphony.

Cataclysmic changes over the preceding decade and a half left everyone looking for new definitions and directions in the 1970s. At Albany State, the Founder's Day observances in 1976 included a series of four symposia dealing with the question of whether predominantly black institutions in the university system could or should continue to exist. Before any scheme to combine Albany State and Albany Junior Colleges could emerge, it was obvious that such a merger would be resisted by forces on both sides of the river.

There were changes in society in the mid-1970s. At local theaters we could see the boom in black exploitation films with features like "Uptown Saturday Night" and "Cleopatra Jones." Richard Roundtree from nearby Thomasville became the first black to star in a dramatic series on TV with his adventure program "Shaft." Mainstream hits included "Blazing Saddles," the Mel Brooks satire on the cowboy film genre. And some of us were among the 4,000 who went to see the first Rolling Stones concert at the Fox Theater in Atlanta. Or maybe that was one of our older children.

Looking back on the mid-seventies, we remember John White's election to the county commission, the first black man elected to the post. Well educated, White was from Alabama and had been a school coun-

selor and TV reporter with WALB. Later, he would become the first black state senator elected from here since Reconstruction. Such "firsts" abounded in Albany in this era.

Other news stories of the seventies that seemed to grab the public's attention included the Alday Murder Case—its investigation, trials, and appeals. Crime seemed to be on everyone's minds in the seventies. This was both a reflection of statistical reality and the fear that haunted us all as social change and international terrorism kept us on edge.

The decade that began with Watergate (1972-73) ended with the hostage crisis in Iran (1980-81). An idealistic presidential candidate from southwest Georgia, Jimmy Carter, instilled renewed pride in the region. But as President, his administration faced runaway oil prices, double-digit inflation, and an interminable hostage situation in Iran. There, U.S. embassy staff and other Americans who had been working or traveling in Iran were held hostage by fundamentalist Muslims under the protection of the government of the Ayatollah Khomeini.

Carter did enjoy success in developing the Camp David Accords, opening the path for better Arab-Israeli relations. If the economy and foreign affairs consumed the Carter presidency, it also prepared the man for his role as an advocate of international cooperation and humane government for decades to come. His stature

as a mediator of international conflict will forever define his place in history. Of course, locals continue to read the newspaper to see if "Jimmy" will be teaching his welcome-all Sunday school class in Plains each week. Sometimes they also encounter him on builds at local Habitat for Humanity projects. An Albanian named Hamilton "Ham" Jordan laid the political strategy that guided Carter to the White House. Jordan and fellow Georgian Lester "Jody" Powell later served on the White House staff. The son of a successful insurance agent, Richard Jordan, "Ham" had grown up here under circumstances that were anything but unusual. It is worth recalling, however, that his sister suffered an attack of polio and nearly died. Her illness was said to have helped form his view of life.

The Carter defeat in the 1980 election was a landslide. Locally, it was a dead heat (13,430 to 12,726 in the county). Afterward, the *Herald* editor posed the question: "What's He Gonna Do Now?" A youthful 56, Carter said he wanted to "return to Plains, open an office, write his memoirs, and become a good fly fisherman." Critics might note that he came home to Atlanta in large part, opened a presidential library near his Emory/Coca-Cola friends, and wrote his memoires. Most underestimated his chances of being elected in the first place. Later, we would be amazed by his brilliant post-presidential career.

Images of the years around 1980 included the film *Raiders of the Lost Ark* (1981), creating a new genre of nostalgic adventure and ushering in two decades of special effects extravaganzas; Herschel Walker winning the Heisman Trophy and propelling Georgia to a national football championship; and discovering that the latest rage, microwave ovens, even at over $300 each, did not make the ideal anniversary present.

Harry James, the trumpeter and husband of Betty Grable (she whose figure graced the noses of so many war planes and whose pictures traveled in many a knapsack during World War II), died in 1983. He had been born on March 15, 1916 to a circus family during a stopover in Albany. His parents were staying at the St. Nicholas Hotel and stayed long enough to have him christened at St. Paul's Episcopal Church, three blocks away.

For some, the 1970s were a grim time as bankruptcies reached an all-time high in Georgia. In 1984, the unemployment rate swelled to 8.5 percent in Georgia and Albany's situation was slightly worse than the average. Some area politicos were outspoken in their opposition to the state lottery under consideration by the state legislature. Senator John White had introduced the measure. Judging from the lottery's current local popularity, many locals probably favored it thinking it might be a chance to get out of debt. The lottery would eventually provide huge resources for the school and university systems, and in the 1990s it would be used for the "Hope" Scholarship Program so that capable students would be assured a place in college with state help.

The Reagan years of the early 1980s brought some luster back to American foreign policy. Reagan negotiated the release of the U.S. hostages in Iran. And his "Star Wars" initiative to position weaponry in space that could interdict a surprise nuclear attack ushered in the new electronic and communications society. This recalls Kennedy's "man on the moon" enterprise that spawned America's technological resurgence in the 1960s. Of course, even the most gifted of politicians can claim to do little more than tell which way the wind is already blowing.

1986 was the 150th anniversary of the founding of the city and it was observed in style. Thronateeska Heritage Center sponsored a beard contest and commissioned artist Oscar Rayneri to create the now unbiquitous-in-print-form collage of area landmarks. In a continuing and inevitable succession of "firsts," Juanita Cribbs became the first African American woman to serve on the County Commission.

The 1990s brought new difficulties to the U.S. abroad: the incident in which terrorists destroyed an airliner over Lockerby, Scotland; the bombing of the American Marine barracks in Beirut; and the drug addiction epidemic that seemed to define the times. "Just say no" was the slogan of the First Lady Nancy Reagan's anti-drug campaign. Military preparedness stimulated some segments of the economy while stifling others.

Health services and post-secondary education are critical to the economy and the future of the city. Shown are the heads of some of the most important institutions in the area during a meeting of the Board of Regents here. Dr. Anthony O. Parker, President of Albanyy Technical Institute; Dr. Stephen Portch, Chancellor of the University System of Georgia's Board of Regents; Dr. Portia Holmes Shields, the new President of Albany State University; Mr. Joel Wernick, Director of Phoebe Putney; and, Dr. Peter Sereno, President of Darton College. ASU photo.

And of course there was the tragedy of the AIDS epidemic that even reached rural southwest Georgia. Denied at first and sometimes callously dismissed as only affecting the most expendible in society, its magnitude would gradually call forth a groundswell of national compassion.

What do we recall swirling about our own times as the new millennium approached? First, the Berlin Wall and then the whole edifice of the Soviet Union collapsed. Miraculously, what we had all feared for so long, what we had come to accept as an unnerving fact of life, suddenly disappeared. Almost overnight, the Cold War ended.

In the 1990s, young adults would become obsessed with physical fitness, careerism, and computers. And they found their sense of community as much in the television sitcoms as in their music. In much of the South, radio stations faced the inevitable: at least regionally, pop music's dominance on the radio dial was over. It had "deconstructed" into "rap," "country," "talk radio," and christian religious programming.

The presidency in the late nineties would be caught up in scandals. Unlike President Warren G. Harding in the 1920s, President Bill Clinton would see his ratings soar in spite of personal immorality. Perhaps the most disturbing news events of the era were the tragic outcome of the Waco Incident, the bombing of the Murrah Federal Building in Oklahoma City, mass suicides, random outbreaks of gun violence on school grounds, and the media feeding frenzy occasioned by the murder trial of former football great O.J. Simpson.

We were still wondering as the 1990s wore down if any of these things were portents of the future or just aberrations. But another 1920s "retro" phenomena cropped up: everybody seemed bent on becoming an expert on investments and the stock market. And strangely, national polls showed that, although most young adults believed that the Social Security System would be bankrupt before they reached retirement age, most also believed that extraterrestrial beings have visited the earth.

This helps explain the popularity of the 1997 movie *Independence Day*, in which aliens arrive to conquer Earth. The President learns that his own government concealed alien visits to Roswell, New Mexico in the post-World War II era. Even serious reporters had been writing about the "Roswell Incident" for a decade or more before the film came out.

But the largest hit at the box office of 1997-98, perhaps of all cinematic history was "Titanic," a romantic retelling of the story of the ill-fated British liner and of the two star-crossed lovers aboard.

For all its diversity, the cable vision business brought us programming that looked a lot like what magazines had brought into our homes in earlier years. For the most part, the mysteries of ancient Egypt, *National Geographic* specials on the recovery of lost cities and ships, and the proliferation of home improvement and "collectibles" programs rounded out the list for adults. Children—especially teenagers— found the lure of MTV and VH1, both music video channels, irresistible. On the old airborne channels of the major networks there were still the continuing permutations of situation comedies and talk shows.

As the century began to wind down, two local controversies attracted statewide attention. One was the dispute over the cutting down what some contended was the "Friendship Oak." The other was the controversy begun when the City Commission renamed Jefferson Street after the martyred civil rights leader, the Reverend Martin Luther King Jr.

As suburban sprawl reached into adjoining Lee County, plans to widen Philema Road came to fruition. The old three-way stop at Philema and Jefferson (Old Leesburg Road) became a bottleneck at rush hour, and the intersection was slated for improvements, including a traffic light. The Department of Transportation granted financial compensation for its planned

The old dining hall on the ASU campus (now renamed for Orene Hall) was flooded in 1994 and beautifully restored afterward. It was protected by sandbags in the Flood of 1998. Photo by Joseph H. Kitchens.

cutting of a large live oak that stood in the way of better traffic flow.

Beginning in the fall of 1992, a group was organized to prevent the destruction of the tree and a debate began over whether the tree was in fact the "Friendship Oak" and also whether it was of an age that would warrant spending more to save it. The lines were drawn between "tree huggers" and safety/progress advocates, with the DOT taking most of the criticism in the press.

When road widening began in May 1994, the Superior Court granted a restraining order blocking the tree's removal, then decided it lacked the authority to intervene. In September 1995, the Georgia Supreme Court likewise temporarily halted the cutting, but later demurred and the case ended up before the U.S. District Court of Judge Louis Sands. He, too, issued a temporary injunction and ordered the DOT to study the historical importance of the tree. This was putting the "fox in the hen house," according to tree defenders. Predictably, DOT found no historical reason to save the tree.

All-night vigils and rallies, placards and banners, and coffee mugs bearing the likeness of the tree all failed to drum up the necessary support for the City Commission to declare the tree a landmark. When Judge Sands lifted the injunction on June 12, 1997, the tree was cut down as soon as the afternoon rush hour ended.

By morning, there was only debris left. Dawson Attorney T. Gamble, who represented the tree's supporters in court, told reporters, "I'm disappointed, but I can go home and sleep knowing we fought on moral ground for what was right." DOT gave the tree's remains to a charitable group raising money for a one-year-old Lee County girl who had undergone a bone marrow transplant.

Perhaps the most interesting aspect of the controversy was that the tree found supporters all over the state. There were regular updates on Georgia Public Radio news and people called from all over the country to inquire about the tree. But there was little support locally. Advocates within city government and the local college community never really emerged. Many, perhaps most, Albanians seemed indifferent. The debate got on to issues of the tree's age and history and how a city rich in trees simply failed to demand

that the tree be preserved. Later, when many of the magnolias and oaks were cut down along Radium Springs Road, there were few public complaints lamenting the lost trees that had helped make Radium such a beautiful area.

The controversy over the renaming of Jefferson Street produced a more widespread and vehement debate. Jefferson is the principle north-south corridor connecting the downtown with the bypass. MLK Drive, a major corridor in south Albany, was to be extended by renaming Jefferson for Georgia's only Nobel Prize winner. Of course, Thomas Jefferson holds a special place in the southern pantheon of heroes. A Virginian, he was the author of the Declaration of Independence, as every school child is taught. His agrarian democratic ideal fit well with the independent-minded suspicion of the federal government. Divisions ran deep.

After months of wrangling, the City Commission, by a narrow margin, voted to change the name of North and South Jefferson Street, so that Martin Luther King Jr. Drive would be continued northward. At this point in time, much of North Jefferson Street's historic fabric had been destroyed. Lawyers' offices dotted the blocks nearest town. Phoebe Putney Hospital, now a regional medical center, and surrounding medical offices were most apparent between First and Fifth avenues. Public attention had been focused earlier on the sale and relocation of one of the Tift family homes from Jefferson Street to a site in Alabama.

Proponents argued that it would unite the city to carry the King name northward. Opponents threatened to move their businesses off Jefferson if the name change was not reversed. It was unpatriotic and violated tradition, they argued, to arbitrarily rename the street.

Former President and Mrs. Jimmy Carter came down to help build houses when the Albany affiliate of Habitat for Humanity (Flint River Habitat for Humanity) began building. On the left is Annie Mae Rhodes. Photo courtesy of Flint River Habitat for Humanity.

The restored Municipal Auditorium, home of the Albany Symphony. Since the national Bicentennial in 1975-76, a number of important buildings in Albany had been renovated in such a way as to protect their historical integrity: In addition to the auditorium and the New Albany Hotel, there are the Albany Railroad Station and the First National Bank (now the Chamber of Commerce). Mt. Zion Church will soon be restored to serve as the Albany-Mount Zion Civil Rights Museum. Photo by Joseph H. Kitchens.

Just before city elections, the new signs went up proclaiming the change to Martin Luther King Jr. Drive. They came down just as quickly when the new commission reversed the sign changes in February of 1997. Down came the new signs, up went the old ones. A supervisor in the city's traffic engineering department told a *Herald* reporter, "We just put'em up and take'em down when they tell us to." He added that the department would keep the King signs ready in the event of another reversal and there the dispute rests for the time being.

Since James Gray Sr. began demolishing the central square's buildings to make room for new development in the 1980s, it has taken almost a decade for new leadership to coalesce and for there to be anything like a consensus on a new plan for the downtown. The flood of 1994 both delayed the emergence of consensus, but it also provided impetus for action.

Flooding is a fact of life in Albany. Dating back to 1841, there are records of repeated floodings. In Nelson Tift's diary there is a brief noting of the flood known as Harrison's freshet, so named because it occurred during the brief presidency of William Henry Harrison. Our area is flat and water is both slow to run off and to be absorbed. While the city sits on a slight bluff, many structures have been built in low-lying

areas to be near the center of town, and in more recent decades to enjoy living alongside creeks and lakes.

More than 50 years after the first recorded flood in 1841, there was a flood in 1897, then more in 1912 and 1913, all more than 10 feet above flood stage. When the river crested at 37.5 feet on January 21, 1925, the city had not experienced a flood of this magnitude in anyone's memory, and, as we have seen, the effects were traumatic. Almost as destructive as the flood of 1925 was the one in 1929 (34.4 feet). Events in 1943, 1944, and 1949 occurred before the city experienced its greatest growth in population and area. From 1960 through 1975, there were six more floods, with the worst coming in 1966 (slightly higher than the 1929 flood). A frequent victim of these floods was Albany State, even after a dike was built to protect the campus following the flood of 1925.

It was the flood of 1966 (34.72) that many Albanians remembered best before Tropical Storm Alberto generated the flood that crested on July 7, 1994, at 44.3 feet. Albany and areas adjoining the Flint River system experienced the worst recorded flood in history. In Albany, 22,000 people were displaced and

The New Albany Hotel has been a landmark in downtown Albany since the nineteenth century (it is the third by the name). Its renovation and transformation into apartments was completed in 1998 and it is now renamed "Albany Heights." Photo by Joseph H. Kitchens.

6,500 buildings damaged. The cost was a staggering $500 million in damages and recovery costs. As in earlier flooding, those most hurt by its effects lived in south Albany, the Radium Springs-Putney area, and along the larger creeks. President Clinton came to Albany to assure the city that federal aid would be forthcoming.

Although only four deaths could be attributed to the torrent, to describe the impact on people's lives would require a much larger book. Homes were lost. Schools became emergency centers. Coffins floated from the downtown cemeteries and were captured in photographs that will forever be etched in our memories. Afterwards, victims faced an endless maze of frustrating paperwork as they found that getting aid was more difficult than anyone imagined. A city flood recovery center was set up at Broad and North Madison to provide additional office space for agencies and non-profit agencies working on relief programs. Neighbors, families, and friends took victims into their homes. City departments faced massive cleanup problems. Accusations of neglected planning flew hot and fast in the newspapers. National media coverage inspired contributions and offers of help. Church volunteers, the Red Cross, the police, and sheriff's departments faced a month of exhausting shifts.

Those who could afford to do so rebuilt along the creeks. Many home sites in south Albany were rebuilt with expensive higher foundations to get them above the levels of the most frequent floods. Some of these rebuilding projects were scarcely finished when the flood of 1998 hit. It could not have been anticipated by much. At 36.9 feet, it was the third worst flood in the city's history after those of 1925 and 1994. Damage was estimated at 25 million dollars. Some of the older structures at ASU were threatened, but by then the main campus sat high above the old one.

Before the 1994 flood, the Albany-Dougherty Inner City Authority, a governmental entity, engaged city business leaders and began a "visioning" process in the early 1990s. Then the flood brought federal disaster relief dollars into the mix. In 1994, a special sales tax referendum in the county generated some funds for both planning and implementing changes. The icing on the cake came in the form of the Federal Intermodal Surface Transportation Enhancement Act (ISTEA) grants to the city. What was missing from the mix at that point was private sector participation to help unlock the city's potential.

Many local leaders helped to organize the group known as Albany Tomorrow Incorporated (ATI), organized in 1995, but the catalyst that got the interaction underway was Dougherty County Attorney Spencer Lee. Convinced that no better opportunity would pre-

"JUNE BUG'S" GROCERY

"June Bug's Grocery," for many years was a South Albany landmark. Photo by Dr. Mary Lawson.

*L*andmarks in the community are not always grand. Just as often, it is our memories of the friends we knew there or just the familiar daily routine of the place that brings it again to mind. In the mid-1950's, Mallory Thomas "Pete" Moulton built a grocery right in the middle of a corn patch. It was known as "Mr. Pete's Store" at first and later as "June Bug's Grocery." This old-timey store became the nucleus of South Albany's African American Community.

The Flood of '94 destroyed the store and the "Cornfield Juke" next door, which had been built in the 1970s. Melvin "June Bug" Griffin, who ran the grocery for several years before the flood, has now opened a mini-plaza shopping center on the same site at the corner of South Madison and Oakridge Drive.

Photo (1987) by Mary Sterner Lawson. Dr. Lawson, an English Professor at ASU, is collecting some of the oral history of South Albany and is the artist of a print of "June Bug's" that graces many local homes.

sent itself in the future, Lee had the persuasiveness and determination to inspire the enthusiasm of key local business leaders. Not since James Gray Sr.'s time has the city seemed so close to a renaissance. Aided by the spectacular growth of the national and state economies, prospects for revitalization seem excellent.

Investigating the success of such river cities as Augusta, Columbus, and Chattanooga, ATI members came to believe that Albany had the key elements for success: a long neglected river front, much of which was already in the hands of government; federal and local government funds to attract private-sector investments; strong, home grown leadership to see the process through; a regional medical center; two colleges; and the vision to break out of the confining glass box of looking only to retail business to help revitalize the downtown. And, from the beginning, the group was biracial and gave opportunities for input

The Government Center. The design was a collaberation between David Maschke Associates and Yielding and Wakeford, Architects. Completed in 1993 it houses both city and county government offices. A new Federal Court House is under construction next door on the Central Square at Broad and Washington.

from the nonprofit sector, particularly Chehaw, the J.W. Jones Ecological Research Center, Thronateeska Heritage Center, and the newly organized Mount Zion-Albany Civil Rights Movement Museum. The experience of other cities suggested that cultural-educational tourism would be a key factor in the success of any revitalization plan.

ATI contracted with Peter Drey, an Atlanta architect, to put together a design-concept group. This team, known as the Albany-on-the-Flint Heritage Team, then guided the process of designing both a revitalized downtown and a user-friendly river front. The plan that emerged from study and public workshops was projected to cost $175 million. Paths for biking and hiking along a river corridor and eventually running from Oakridge Drive in the south to Chehaw Park in the north, the plan projected, would connect to a newly redeveloped downtown, possibly with a modern hotel-convention facility.

Later, Dr. Lindsay Boring of the J.W. Jones Ecological Research Center headed a study group to examine the possibility of a river center. The center would interpret the river, its natural history, our wetlands, and the aquifer system that lies beneath our feet. It would provide a tourist destination site and create new learning opportunities for area schools and colleges.

Eventually, the state legislature provided several million dollars for planning studies to develop the center. Urbanization, fertilizers, insecticides, municipal runoff, and pesticides all pose problems in water stewardship, and a river center seems a perfect way to link the romance and history of the river with the recreational opportunities of the hiking-biking trails, while building a public knowledge base to insure future conservation.

Downtown redevelopment, the river front corri-

dor's recreational opportunities, and the proposed river center are all in the future, of course. And the future is all conjecture. It is heartening, however, to see that the city still produces women and men who have the imagination to dream of a better future.

There is much to celebrate in the city at present. As this is being written, Thronateeska Heritage Center has just completed its renovation and opened its new permanent exhibit. The Mount Zion-Albany Civil Rights Movement Museum is undergoing the same process. The Albany Museum of Art, under Tim Close's leadership, is about to expand, and The Albany Symphony and Theater Albany are flourishing. Chehaw, under a professionalized staff led by Steve Marshall is now accredited and is easily the most popular visitor site in the area. Albany State has become a university and is undergoing the most extensive physical improvements in its history. It is safe to say that the cost of all improvements in the school's history does not equal in cost those of the past three years.

Recovery from the flood of 1994 is largely complete, and the Flint River affiliate of Habitat for Humanity has given new expression to the spiritual values of the community in using hundreds of volunteers to construct affordable housing for those in need. The "Good Life City" could well be renamed the "Volunteer City." The renovation of the old New Albany Hotel has been completed. It is now an apartment building known as Albany Heights. A new federal courthouse is under construction on the southeast corner of the main square. It seems a good time to celebrate our recent accomplishments and to look with optimism to the future. ⊷

AFTERWORD

*W*e have benefited from the help and earlier work of many people and institutions in writing this book. We could never have done this in a timely fashion had it not been for the writers of earlier books about Albany, Dougherty County, Georgia, and the South. Unfortunately, most such works typically were written long ago or have not covered the more recent past. It is good to remember that the Civil War began only 24 years after the founding of the city. Half our history has occurred since 1917.

The files of the *Albany Herald* have been convenient to us here and at the University of Georgia. Time would not permit gleaning from the treasure trove of the various other local newspapers that have served the community. It would be a great boon to researchers if the *Herald* were indexed. The vertical reference files of the Dougherty Public Library were also useful for looking up Herald articles by topic.

Many articles in the *Journal of Southwest Georgia History* were consulted. When the *Journal* was begun, the number of articles in the *Georgia Historical Quarterly* about Southwest Georgia could be counted on one hand. Thronateeska, with the help of business contributors, has done a wonderful thing in continuing this publication, the worth of which will be appreciated by future researchers. Dr. Lee Formwalt, editor of the *Journal*, has been generous in correcting some of our factual errors and pointing us toward valuable materials.

Though usually not at hand for casual readers, there is a growing body of unpublished material on Southwest Georgia in the form of dissertations at various universities. Academic study has tended to focus on black history. This is primarily because of the very dense slave population here in the antebellum period as well as trends toward the use of quantitative analysis.

There is much more research and writing to be done. We are all guilty of citing history to prop up our social theories, advertise our pedigree, or explain why we deserve some privilege or other. It would be much more profitable to actually understand our past as a community and to find in that past both hope born of adversity and a community of understanding.

It is appropriate that Steve Gurr and I have finally written something together. We have been colleagues, friends, and sounding boards for each other for 30 years. (Can it have been so long?) I appreciate his willingness to help and his skill in doing so. We both appreciate all those kind souls who patiently answered our questions. And we both regret that all those who offered to be interviewed could not be, simply because our time ran out.

Would you take some time to record your recollections? They are the cloth from which history is woven.

— Joseph H. Kitchens, Jr.
Albany, Georgia

PART II

CHAPTER VI

PRE-WORLD WAR II

A City By The River Rises

W. T. Lockett Central Feed and Sale Stable. The years following the turn of the century were a time of transition. Horses and mules continued to be an important part of daily life in Southwest Georgia, despite the advent of automobiles. This building stood where the Gordon Hotel (Water, Gas and Light Commission) now stands on Broad. Photo by H.S. Holland.

Sunnyland Farms

When Harry Willson met the future Jane Willson on a train going from Boston to Georgia in 1941, neither one envisioned that together they would create a catalog business that would sell more pecans and other nuts than any other catalog company in the country. Today, Sunnyland Farms is in its fifth decade of operation and boasts a satisfied, loyal clientele from throughout the United States.

"We met on a train coming home for Christmas holidays. I was going to Harvard Business School and she was going to Wellesley College," Willson explains. "We had a lot of time to talk since trains take longer than planes."

Jane and Harry Willson, founders of Sunnyland Farms.

The mail order company was launched in 1948 when a Wellesley alumnae group asked the Willsons to provide pecans for a fund-raiser. They agreed, and the project was quite successful. They began to think of selling pecans as a business venture worth developing.

"We took out an ad in the *New York Times* and started out small," Mrs. Willson says. "We thought that other people might be interested in buying fresh pecans conveniently through mail order, too."

They consulted with an advertising agency on the packaging and marketing needed to launch Sunnyland Farms, Inc. Today, the couple has developed a unique combination of mail order and pecan expertise to handle those decisions.

"I write the catalog copy and she does the layout. We collaborate on what items to feature, and I do most of the purchasing and the finance," Willson says.

"We complement each other's natural talents," agrees Mrs. Willson. "It just kind of works out that way."

The Willsons moved to Albany in 1951 to run the family farm which Harry's father had bought in 1925. Pecans at that time were not a reliable enterprise, so Harry fenced the property and started a cattle operation. Jane nurtured the mail order business as children and time allowed. Early success in marketing required Harry to search Georgia's back roads for the best pecans he could find. (Although 14,000 of Dougherty County's estimated 300,000 pecan trees are grown by Willson Farming Company, a companion operation, they are used only if they are good enough to meet the criteria of selling "only the best of each crop.")

In the 1960s, Willson found he spent most of the fall on the road searching for the best pecans to sell through the mail order business, a project that the family still treated as a sideline. In 1967, he declared, "Either we get in and make it a go or we get out."

"So we got in," Mrs. Willson recalls.

Packing Friendship Tins.

At that time, the customer base was about 5,000. Business doubled during each of the next five years and continues to grow modestly today. Although no figures are released for the privately held company, the company is ranked as the world's top shipper of pecans by mail.

As the customer base grew, so did offerings available through the mail. Today, pecan candies, nut mixes, cookies, dried fruits and nuts of many varieties, gift tins, and home boxes are available through the mail. The original philosophy of providing the very best products available, however, remains unchanged.

"People buy from us sight unseen and on faith. We want always to be sure they aren't disappointed," says Mrs. Willson. She adds, "What people are really buying is Harry's ability to get the very best nuts."

This goal of providing the best product and customer service is the keystone of the entire organization, beginning with the farming operation to the shelling plant, the candy kitchen and toasting room, the packing and shipping departments, and to the office staff that has actual contact with the customers.

Despite this growth, however, the Willsons are not ivory tower executives. Mrs. Willson recalls a time during the 1970s when retired Sunnyland Vice President Calvin Tucker shocked a visiting salesman as he greeted him in work clothes while standing beside a tractor.

"You're the vice president?" the salesman asked.

"Yes, and that's the president down there under the tractor," Tucker replied, pointing to Willson, who was hard at work on a repair. This "hands-on" management continues to insure that both Willsons stay aware of the daily operations as well as planning for long-term goals.

Today, one son, Larry Willson, remains with the company, running various plants and buying the three to four million pounds of pecans required by Sunnyland's operations above and beyond those grown by Willson Farming Co. Three other Willson children have not stayed in the family business but are successful executives and professionals in Atlanta and Philadelphia.

Sunnyland customers, many of whom have become loyal, long-term friends, have watched the family grow along with the business. In 1960, Willson wrote a small note at the bottom of the letter he sent with their catalog. The note stated that

Loading truck.

Jane was helping him again after the birth of their fourth child, their only daughter. Many of the customers sent congratulations and even gifts, so the next year he wrote a few more words about the family at the bottom of the catalog. Today, the Willson Family Update and the updates on many of the Sunnyland Farms/Willson Farming employees are the first-read feature of the catalog.

The Willsons look forward to continuing to sell their products by mail and to enjoy the challenges and rewards of the business. And continuing to keep in touch with their loyal customers, friends they've met through the mail. ❧

Sunnyland Farms has been in business since 1948.

Bobs Candy

After service in the army during World War I, Robert E. "Bob" McCormack returned to Birmingham, Alabama, itching to start his own candy company. He had worked as a teenager at a Nashville, Tennessee, candy store for two years, and then, after graduation from St. Bernard College, for Martin Biscuit Company in Birmingham. He criss-crossed the South looking for a town in which to start his enterprise. A chance remark on a train, "Why don't you check out Albany? It's an up-and-coming place," led him to southwest Georgia.

McCormack liked the town of 11,500 people and decided to start "The Famous Candy Company" there. In May, 1919, he began production with just four other employees. In spite of a sugar shortage in its first year, The Famous Candy Company was successful in making a general line of candies, including coconut, peanut, hard candy, stick candy, and taffy.

A year later, the business was going so well that Bob Mills, an associate from Martin Biscuit Company, came from Birmingham to assume the administrative duties and allow McCormack to devote more time to production and sales. Mills and McCormack bought out the other investors and renamed the company Mills-McCormack Candy Company. Then, since both owners were named Bob, in 1924 the company name was changed to "The Bobs' Candy Company." The proper placement of the apostrophe became a hassle, and it was soon dropped altogether.

In 1926, Bob Mills' interest in the company was bought by Albany accountant James Magill. Bob McCormack's father, Michael, moved to Albany to become bookkeeper and treasurer of the company.

Throughout its history, innovation has made Bobs a leader in the candy industry. In the 1920s Bobs was one of the first candy manufacturers to wrap its products in cellophane, which at that time was imported from France. Taking advantage of the abundant pecan production in the Albany area, Bobs was the first candy manufacturer to use pecans in low-priced candy bars.

During the 1930s, another abundant southwest Georgia crop became important to production at Bobs. Peanuts were used not only in candy, but also in peanut butter cracker sandwiches and salted peanuts, which Bobs began producing.

It was during this period that McCormack made one of his greatest discoveries—right in his own family. Father Harding Keller was a Catholic priest from Arkansas and the brother of McCormack's wife, the former Louise Keller. Father Keller's hobby was tinkering with machinery, a hobby he indulged at his brother-in-law's candy factory when he visited on summer vacations. Father Keller eventually received five patents for machinery he invented for Bobs.

In the mid-1930s, Keller invented a machine which automatically deposited peanut butter on the cracker. Over the next few years the machine was improved and refined so that it made the completed cracker sandwiches.

The final new, sophisticated machine was finished in Arkansas in early 1940 and scheduled for delivery to Bobs on February first. By a stroke of luck, Father Keller's trip to Albany was delayed by a month.

On February 10, 1940, at 4 a.m., a tornado ripped through the business section of Albany, completely destroying the building that had been Bobs Candy Company. The company's casualty insurance did not cover tornados. This total destruction could easily have

been the end of Bobs, but McCormack was determined to resurrect his business. And his reputation as a man of integrity paid off. As trucks carried away the debris of his plant and McCormack struggled to set up a temporary office, he began to hear from suppliers who let him know they would extend a line of credit for as long as he needed to get started again. Buyers wired and called to tell him they would be ready to buy again as soon as he had products to sell.

The delay of Father Keller's peanut butter cracker machine enabled McCormack to have the peanut department at Bobs back in production at a new location just three weeks after the tornado. The entire company was back in business in just five months.

But McCormack never forgot the generosity others showed him in his time of need. As soon as his business was back on its feet, Bob McCormack began a policy, continued to this day, of giving as much as possible to nonprofit causes. In addition, Bobs donated large amounts of candy to various charities throughout the year.

During the 1940s, the three children of the founder came into the business: Bob Jr. in production, Anna Louise in finance, and Bee in personnel and packaging.

While many things have remained the same at Bobs, the product line has changed drastically since the early days. That shift in focus can be directly attributed to Father Keller's development in 1949 of a machine to automatically twist and cut stick candy. Within a few years this machine enabled Bobs to take a decisive lead in the stick candy business.

Soon after the Keller machine was in operation, a machine was developed at Bobs to automatically bend candy sticks into candy canes. Then Bob Jr. and Bee perfected the first boxes and cases to safely pack and ship candy canes on a national basis. In effect, Bobs had created a whole new branch of the national candy industry—candy canes.

In February of 1963, founder Bob McCormack retired as president of the company and turned the reins over to his son, a graduate of the U.S. Naval Academy and veteran of World War II. Bob Jr.'s more relaxed executive style would lead his family business into a new era of growth and expansion. Anna Louise and Bee now held key positions as secretary-treasurer and vice president.

In 1968, Bobs moved from downtown Albany, where it had operated for 49 years, to a new plant on Oakridge Drive. By this time Bobs had become the world's largest manufacturer of candy canes, and hard candy had become the only product of the company.

As candy cane sales grew, it became necessary to begin producing them earlier and earlier each year. This meant the product needed to be stored for many months before the Christmas season. Large warehouses were needed in which the temperature and humidity could be carefully controlled.

To handle this storage, as well as increased production, the Oakridge Drive plant was expanded three times to a total of 375,000 square feet.

During the 1980s, a third generation of McCormacks came into the company: Bob Jr.'s children Mary Helen Dykes, Gregory McCormack, and Julie Roth. Gregory worked first in production; then he undertook research and set up a subsidiary Bobs plant in Jamaica.

In 1989, Bob Jr. retired, and Gregory became the third president of Bobs Candies, Inc. His sisters, like their aunts before them, assumed the key roles of secretary-treasurer and vice president. Under this new young leadership, Bobs has expanded greatly in sales and employment. It continues to be the innovator and leader in its field.

In 1990, at its annual meeting in Denver, Colorado, the National Aeronautical and Space Agency inducted Bobs Candies into the Space Technology Hall of Fame for its role in the application of NASA space technology to commercial use. Bobs was the smallest company ever to receive this honor. The technology applied was "heat pipes," a system developed to transfer warmth from the sun-heated side of a spacecraft to the shaded cold side. Working with NASA, Bobs undertook the first nonspace installation of these heat pipes to humidify the company's warehouses. The experiment was successful, and Bobs saved 30 percent on one of its biggest operating expenses, energy bills.

In 1997 Bobs Candies was named Georgia Family Business of the Year in its class by the Family Enterprise Center of Kennesaw State University. And in 1998, Gregory McCormack, president of Bobs, was selected by *Georgia Trend* magazine as one of the 100 most influential Georgians. ❧

Phoebe Putney Memorial Hospital

A man's desire to honor the memory of his mother back at the turn of the century has proved to be a gift that has benefited the people of Albany and southwest Georgia for nearly a century.

Phoebe nurses in front of the hospital, circa 1925. Phoebe trained many nurses in its Nursing Training School from 1918 until 1934. The original two-year training program was expanded to include a year's rotation at Cincinnati General Hospital in Ohio.

(inset) Phoebe Putney Memorial Hospital's name is dedicated in memory of Judge Francis Flagg Putney's mother—Phebe Putney.

Judge Francis F. Putney was among the founding fathers of a town eight miles south of Albany in the late 1800s. Near his Hardaway Plantation, the streets and lots of the town of Putney were platted. It was the first "colony town" in the area.

As early as February, 1904, Drs. William L. Davis Jr. and W.P. Rushin launched a drive to build a hospital for Albany. They canvassed Dougherty County, selling stock and collecting contributions. They raised $4,000.

Women of Albany also wanted to help establish a hospital for the town, so on October 13, 1905, a group organized the Ladies Hospital Aid Association. Members included Eugenia Gunn Davis (Mrs. Joseph

S. Davis, who was elected president; Janie Godwin Mayo (Mrs. Zachary Mayo), vice president; Nora J. Jones (Mrs. Sidney Johnson Jones), secretary; Annie Smith Davis (Mrs. William L. Davis Jr.), treasurer; and Mrs. Chester M. Clark and Mrs. William Edgar Rowsey were elected chairwomen of the children's ward. They and others like the Ladies at Home, a local branch of the Negro Women's Federation, went to work planning bazaars, dances, carnivals, and tag days that would involve the whole community. The ladies reasoned that, while not everyone could afford to buy stock in the hospital, most people could afford to buy a jar of pickles or spend 25 cents on a ticket to a dance.

Dedicated citizens throughout the community were working hard to accomplish their goal of a hospital for Albany, but it was Judge Putney who made the dream a reality.

Although she did not know him, Mrs. Clark asked Judge Putney for a donation. In a letter to Hospital Aid Association President Mrs. Joseph S. Davis on November 2, 1909, Judge Putney made a generous offer.

If hospital supporters would agree to three conditions, he would give them $25,000 to build the hospital.

"It is the desire of myself and wife," he wrote, "to give a sum of money to some good object that will benefit the greatest number of people as a memorial to my dear mother. We can think of no more worthy object than a substantial aid to the hospital, for which

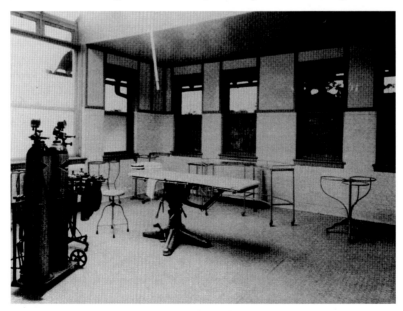

The Palaemon L. Hilsman Operating Room in the original Phoebe, 1934.

the ladies of Albany have been working assiduously for the last few years, to get the necessary funds for this object."

Among Judge Putney's demands, he insisted the hospital be constructed of brick, to make it fireproof, and that "his" hospital serve both races—an idea that stood out in stark contrast to the prevailing practice in a South where memories of the Civil War and Reconstruction were still fresh. His first stipulation was perhaps the simplest; Judge Putney asked that the hospital be named in memory of his mother, Phebe Putney.

Mrs. Davis did not hesitate. On November 3, members of the Ladies Hospital Aid Association and a number of Albany physicians gathered at the Carnegie Library to hear Judge Putney's proposal. They accepted his offer immediately. Within two days, the hospital's Board of Control, with Judge Putney as its chairman, decided to build a new brick hospital rather than renovate a building the Hospital Aid Association owned. It would serve all, regardless of race or circumstances.

On July 31, 1911, a grand opening for Phoebe Putney Memorial Hospital was held. (On her tombstone, Phebe Putney's name omits the "o" in Phoebe, but from the earliest records, the name of the hospital dedicated to her memory was spelled "Phoebe." The reason for the discrepancy has been lost with the decades.) The hospital officially opened August 1.

Sixteen patients were admitted during Phoebe's first month of operation. A regional hospital from the beginning, these patients came to Phoebe from as far away as Baker, Miller, Worth, and Crisp Counties. In its first year, 189 patients were admitted and doctors performed 91 operations.

Phoebe's focus embraced the region and beyond, even in the earliest days. Thirty-nine percent of the first year's admissions were from Georgia counties other than Dougherty.

This is just one of many traditions from the hospital's

past that continues today. In 1997, 45 percent of the hospital's admissions came from outside Dougherty County and 520,000 people were served through the Phoebe system.

More importantly, however, is the hospital's continuing commitment to serving all in need.

Today, the Phoebe family is a dynamic community of more than 2,600 employees. Phoebe's Heart, Cancer, Emergency, Women's, and Neonatal centers are the core of a comprehensive regional medical complex where state-of-the-art technology bonds with state-of-the-heart care.

Eighty-seven years after its founding, Phoebe Putney Health Systems, Inc. is preparing to enter the new millennium with a strengthened commitment to its founding mission. The labor, dedication, sacrifice, and loyalty of Phoebe's employees, board members, physicians, and community volunteers—past, present, and future—insure for posterity that citizens in need will always find accessible, affordable, quality health care at Phoebe. ❧

Much of the preceding has been taken from A History from the Heart, *the history of Phoebe Putney Memorial published by Phoebe in 1993. Used with permission.*

The completion of an expansion in 1993 signaled the beginning of a new era in regional health care . . . reaffirming the hospital's commitment to providing the finest health care services to residents of southwest Georgia.

(inset) Today, Phoebe's innovative services include most specialties and subspecialties and are supported by state-of-the-art technology ensuring world-class health care, but it is the Phoebe staff's caring hands that have earned Phoebe the reputation as "the hospital with a heart."

Kimbrell-Stern Funeral Directors

*A*s children, E.J. "Buck" Stern Jr. and his best friend, W.R. "Bob" Kimbrell, loved hanging around the local funeral home. "Back then, the funeral homes had ambulance service," Stern says. "We'd hear the ambulances and get on our bicycles and try to follow them. What else could you do in a small town?"

What the pair didn't know at the time was that their shared curiosity would one day manifest itself into ownership of one of Albany's longest continually operating family businesses, Kimbrell-Stern Funeral Directors.

"We knew the ambulances were kept at the funeral home, and we just started hanging around," Stern recalls. "We'd do just about anything for excitement."

The funeral business that would one day become Kimbrell-Stern was established by the Wilder family in 1880 as the Albany Undertaking Co. It was later purchased by Mr. and Mrs. C. W. Thomas.

Kimbrell and Stern's continual presence at the funeral home paid off when they were just 12 years old. The Thomases offered the duo jobs, and they began working afternoons and weekends at the former Albany Undertaking Co.

"They paid us a quarter every week," Stern recalls. "With that much money we could go to the Liberty Theater, see a movie, and buy a coke and a hot dog."

Over the years, Kimbrell-Stern Funeral Directors' owners have adhered to the founder's goal of providing the most comprehensive funeral services available in southwest Georgia, and the newest generation of owners is no exception.

"I really think Mrs. Thomas was trying to get rid of us," Stern jokes.

While lunch and an afternoon matinee polished off the 25 cents Kimbrell and Stern earned as "gophers" for the funeral home, Stern recalled the Christmas of 1937, when the Thomases bought the boys their first suits.

"We worked for them while we were in high school, and as time went by we got more and more involved in things," Stern says.

"Our family was criticized for letting kids hang around the funeral home, but our parents never discouraged us."

Kimbrell and Stern served a two-year apprenticeship with the funeral home before going to mortuary college. Kimbrell was the first to go to mortuary college, attending the Cincinnati College of Embalming.

World War II broke out in December of 1941, and after Kimbrell finished mortuary college he enlisted in the Navy. Stern wanted to follow his lifelong friend into the Navy, but couldn't. So instead, Stern enlisted at Turner Field Army Air Corps in Albany, also in 1942.

Each completed his tour of duty in 1946, and then Stern attended the Cincinnati College of Embalming.

Meanwhile, Stern's younger brother, Charles,

joined Albany Undertaking Co., and in 1950, the three bought the Thomases' interest in the company and formed Kimbrell-Stern. The younger Stern was a partner in the business until his death in 1981.

It was under the leadership of Kimbrell and the Stern brothers that the company became incorporated and moved from its original Broad Avenue location to its current one on Dawson Road in 1964.

"When I started in the funeral service, a majority of the funerals were done in the homes, and embalming a lot of times was done in the homes too," Stern says.

Albany Undertaking Co. installed the first electric organ in south Georgia in 1936. It was featured on WGPC radio and later was donated to the Thronateeska Heritage Foundation, according to Stern.

Part of the history of Kimbrell-Stern is the tradition of the business being passed on to people closely associated with the business. It was no exception when it came time for Kimbrell and Stern to give up control of the business after more than 100 years of combined service.

Four successors, all long-time employees, purchased the business on April 13, 1990.

"It has always passed on to personnel connected with this organization," Stern says. "We just felt like local people could serve local people better than a large public company."

David M. Stern, Robert L. "Bucky" Brokkshier Jr., William I. "Billy" Coleman Jr., and S.S. "Sandy"

Mackey Jr. are the new generation of leaders at Kimbrell-Stern.

Kimbrell retired in 1990, while Stern retired a year later. Despite his retired status, Stern can still be found hanging around the funeral home on any given day of the week, now as a volunteer.

"I can't get it out of my blood," Stern says.

In 1950, when Kimbrell and the Sterns took over, the company was performing about 200 funerals a year; today, Kimbrell-Stern performs between 325 and 350 funerals a year and offers an expanded line of service.

With the 1985 purchase of Crown Hill Cemetery, Kimbrell-Stern began providing mortuary facilities, funeral services, and memorial services as well as burial sites. Kimbrell-Stern also installed Albany's first crematorium in 1985. Throughout the business's years, its owners have adhered to the founder's goal of providing the most comprehensive funeral services available in southwest Georgia.

And the newest generation of owners is no exception.

"We've all had deaths in our families, so we've experienced what people who are coming here to see us have experienced," Secretary-Treasurer Billy Coleman says.

"We offer understanding, compassionate, courteous, sympathetic service." ❧

The funeral business that would one day become Kimbrell-Stern was established by the Wilder family in 1880 as the Albany Undertaking Co., and was later purchased by Mr. and Mrs. C. W. Thomas.

Hall-ing Refuse Co.

L. N. "Red" Hall, a talented athlete, dreamed of playing baseball in the major leagues. He was a two-sport letterman at the University of Alabama, playing both basketball and baseball before graduating in 1922.

While he never realized his dream of playing professional baseball, Hall did end up batting "cleanup," working for the City of Albany as director of sanitation and later establishing his own sanitation company.

In 1959, about a year before Hall's retirement from the City of Albany, he bought "an old antiquated garbage truck" and became an entrepreneur, according to Richard "Dick" Martin, who married Hall's granddaughter.

Hall convinced Martin to come run the company for him, eventually buying the company and expanding the business tremendously. "After Mr. Hall's retirement, he ran the company until I came in September of '76," Martin says. "I came here with the purpose of buying the business. After six months, Mr. Hall financed me and I bought it."

According to Martin, when he came to the company it had only "half a commercial dumpster route," and he defined that as about a half a day's work. "We had three industrial routes and no residential customers at

all," he says. "We had an old two-room trailer office on Old Radium Springs Road, and a secretarial bookkeeper, no radios in the trucks, one mechanic, and maybe five drivers."

In the early years, Martin estimates that 85 percent of the business was strictly industrial. Over the years, industry put more and more emphasis on recycling, reducing the amount of waste it generated. This change led to a metamorphosis of the business, as explained by Martin.

With the new growth in business, the office and operations were relocated from their site on Old Radium Springs to a newer and larger facility on Pecan Lane in 1983.

The business began expanding into residential service on, what was at first, a small scale. "Now we had a total reversal in our business," he says. "As the community of southwest Georgia has grown, so has our residential business, and our commercial dumpster accounts have continued to grow tremendously. However, industrial customers now account for only a small part of the business."

The company began offering residential curbside pickup in 1986, with one truck, two employees, and no customers, Martin recalls. They have now grown to service more than 37,000 residential customers.

At present Hall-ing Refuse boasts 104 employees, 47 garbage trucks, and a dominant business of solid waste collection and Port-o-let services in 13 southwest Georgia counties.

Also in 1986, Hall-ing Refuse entered into a partnership with Waste Management Inc.—the country's largest waste service company. As a Waste Management partner, Hall-ing Refuse was eligible to receive a broad range of operational support services, such as equipment specifications and purchasing, assistance in route planning, maintenance programs, sales and safety programs, and employee engineering, as well as financial support.

"We have worked hard to build our reputation of reliable, dependable service with customer satisfaction as our number one priority," Martin says.

The partnership with Waste Management enabled the company to continue to provide its customers with a level of service that was nothing less than great, as expressed by Martin. "That's what we believe partnership is all about . . . going through it together, even when the going may sometimes get tough or the unexpected comes up."

After years of continued success, Martin eventually reclaimed full ownership of Hall-ing Refuse, later selling the company to a rapidly growing corporation, Allied Waste of Scottsdale, Arizona, in March 1998. However, the reputation of Hall-ing Refuse as a company of exceptional service and fair business continues on. ❧

Howard, Ventulett & Bishop Insurors Inc.

*(left to right)
Thomas E. Bishop,
Jack M. Howard,
and John P.
Ventulett, Jr.*

oward, Ventulett & Bishop Insurors Inc. is Albany's oldest continuous business.

Originally established in 1847 by Captain John A. Davis as the Davis Insurance Co., the agency has changed names from time to time due to the addition and deletion of partners, but the firm remains that of the original.

Throughout its history, the agency has paid thousands of claims, but one claim payment made insurance history.

In 1861, the Byington Hotel, located in downtown Albany, was destroyed by fire. Insured by Captain Davis through the Hartford Insurance Co —a company that today is still part of the Howard, Ventulett & Bishop Insurors' family—the claim check of $4,948 arrived in Albany in the last mail to clear the lines as the War Between the States began.

The check now rests in the archives of Hartford Insurance Co. Howard, Ventulett & Bishop Insurors has been a representative of Hartford Insurance Co. since its founding in 1854.

Currently the owners and officers of Howard, Ventulett & Bishop Insurors are Jack M. Howard, president; John P. Ventulett Jr., vice president; and Thomas E. Bishop, vice president.

Jack M. Howard, president, received his Bachelor of Business Administration degree from the University of Georgia. He received his Certified Insurance Counselor designation in 1987.

John P. Ventulett Jr., vice president, a graduate of Georgia State University, has had family connections with this insurance agency dating back to 1901. The business was then referred to as Ventulett and Davis. John P. Ventulett earned his Certified Insurance Counselor's license in 1983.

Thomas E. Bishop, vice president, received his Bachelor of Science Degree from the University of Georgia, and a Master of Insurance from Georgia State University. He has earned his Associate in Risk Management and holds the professional designation of Chartered Property Casualty Underwriter.

Over the years the firm has made numerous acquisitions—two of the largest were the Pace Insurance in 1991 and Warren & Brimberry and Walden & Kirkland Insurors in 1997.

Today, the agency provides risk management, insurance solutions, expert counsel, and professional service to individuals and businesses throughout the country. Howard, Ventulett & Bishop is committed to excellence in service to their clients, companies, and customers. ❧

City of Albany

A defining moment in the city's history, the flood of 1994 forced the evacuation of over 14,000 residents from their homes and caused untold damage to lives and property.

Mother Nature has been Albany's friend and its nemesis. Founded on the banks of the Flint River, Albany was established to facilitate the selling and exporting of cotton.

A group of investors from Hawkinsville came up with a plan to help local farmers market the cotton that would become the South's principal cash crop. Their idea was to build a community on the west bank of the Flint River, which joins the Chattahoochee River, and at Apalachicola finds the Gulf of Mexico. To implement this plan, the investors hired 25-year-old Nelson Tift. A native of Groton, Connecticut, Tift arrived in the future city on October 13, 1836. He sketched out a "checkerboard" town plan and named the city Albany. The geography of this new town reminded Tift of the Hudson River valley, where the city of Albany, New York, lies.

From its earliest days, Albany's economy was diverse and included agriculture, commerce, manufacturing, and shipping. That still holds true today, and that diversity has helped the city serve as the hub of southwest Georgia.

"I think Albany has always had the role of the leading city in southwest Georgia," City Manager Janice Allen Jackson says. "What is new, is now we're approaching the status of a leading city of the state."

Per capita retail sales in Albany rank second only to those of Atlanta; in 1994 and 1995 Albany led the state

in announced expansions at some of its largest industries; and in 1998, the city was being courted as a possible site for an ice hockey franchise. But all of that was, for a second, nearly lost in 1994, when the Flint River spilled its banks and flooded a majority of the city. At the height of the flood when the river crested at 43 feet—23 feet above flood stage—18,000 families were evacuated, more than 5,000 homes and buildings were damaged, and some entire sections of the city were underwater, submerged in as much as 12 feet of water.

Things looked grim indeed as the murky waters of the Flint began to recede, but from the devastation arose a community spirit, the likes of which the town had never seen.

"People whose own property had been destroyed were at the Civic Center making sandbags to stop that from happening to others," Jackson says. While the river's destructive power will not soon be forgotten, city leaders are pinning hopes for Albany's future on the Flint. A multimillion-dollar downtown/riverfront development project is underway, and according to Jackson, when complete, Albany will be a first tier Georgia city.

"I think Albany is a community of tremendous potential," Jackson says. "We're only beginning to tap that potential." ❧

Consolidated Loan Co.

118 N. Jackson Street. Both 128 Court Avenue and this location were demolished in 1980 for the Central Square.

Charlie Jones, the founder of Consolidated Loan Co., was fond of saying that he began his business in "Taxi Smith's coal bin with a notebook for a ledger and a cigar box for a cash drawer."

Charles M. Jones was born in Virginia, married and had a son in El Paso, and in 1930 was working as a CPA in a loan company in Tampa. That same year, Mr. Jones chose Albany to open his own office. There was no loan company, and Albany is beautiful in the spring. The opening was April 30, 1930.

Shortly afterward a group of local businessmen headed by W.F. Jefferson opened another company, but they soon merged under the name of Consolidated Loan and Finance Company. Mr. Jones subsequently bought out the other partners. The business was first located at Pine and Court Avenue in a building that was later Albany First Federal Savings and then Robinson-Humphrey, Inc.

The company prospered under the leadership of Mr. Jones and his Board of Directors, who were Jim Bush, Clerk of Court; Dan L. Gibson, Postmaster; H.B. "Buck" Stovall, Merchant; and C.L. Neuman, President of Albany Trust and Banking.

In 1936 they moved to larger quarters on Court Avenue, and the first branch was opened in Thomasville with J.A. Curry as manager. In 1944 Curry became a partner and helped open a branch in Cairo. Both of these offices began in locations above five-and-ten-cent stores and moved later to ground floor offices.

Charles Jones Jr. returned from school and World War II in 1948 and joined the company. The fourth office was opened in Fitzgerald in 1959. In 1960 the Albany office moved to N. Jackson, and the first American Finance Company was opened on Court Avenue and later on Broad.

In 1971 Mr. Jones passed away, and Charles Jones III, "Chuck," joined the company. Mr. Curry's interests were purchased in 1982 when he retired. Mr. Jones Jr. and Mr. Jones III worked together until Mr. Jones Jr.'s retirement in 1992.

Seven new offices have been opened since 1988: Consolidated and American in Macon and Columbus, and Consolidated in Douglasville, Dublin, and Americus. Longtime Vice President Jim Adams heads the mortgage loan department in each of them.

Good citizenship and civic responsibility have been hallmarks of the Joneses and are encouraged in all offices. Each branch has a history and stories to tell. Their founder would have been proud. ❧

The opening of the "new" office on Court Avenue in 1953. (left to right) Charles M. Jones, J.G. Downey, Annette Halstead (Urquhart), Charles M. Jones Jr., R.B. "Dick" Bowman, Bill Wilson, Aubrey Sileo, Ruth Varnadore (Stewart), and Effie Williamson (Weaver).

Dougherty County Commission

Nestled in the heart of Georgia's plantation country, Dougherty County is known as the "Quail Capital of the World."

Created by an act of the Georgia General Assembly on December 15, 1853, Dougherty County was named for Charles Dougherty of Athens, Georgia, a noted antebellum lawyer and jurist and a strong advocate of states' rights.

Dougherty County was cut out of its neighbor to the south, Baker County, according to longtime commission chairman Gil Barrett.

"Dougherty County was founded as a farming hub," Barrett says, "and boats would haul cotton up and down the Flint River."

The Flint River, which runs through Dougherty County, has helped define much of the county's past, and county leaders are looking to the river to help define its future.

Dougherty County Commission Chairman Gil Barrett.

Over the years, the river has helped Dougherty County evolve from a farming hub into an industrial hub, housing plants for some of the nation's largest manufacturers like Procter & Gamble, Merck & Co., and Miller Brewing Co.

"I have seen so many changes since I first came on board 40 years ago," Barrett says. "The county budget 40 years ago was $520,000. Today, the total county budget is over $37 million, and that's not counting what the county spends on special local option sales tax."

With a population around 95,000, Dougherty County has experienced tremendous growth in government services, including a sheriff's department that has grown from five deputies and four or five jailers to 40 deputies and 178 jailers, according to Barrett.

When Barrett first joined the commission in 1958, an elderly gentleman, Tom Fleming, served as the clerk of Dougherty County, Barrett recalls. Fleming kept the minutes for county commission meetings and did the county's payroll—administrative jobs that today employ seven people, plus a county administrator and an assistant.

With an expanding industrial and retail base, Barrett credits available land, cheap taxes, and the county's leadership working together with Dougherty County's success.

As evidence of that success, Barrett points to the Marine Corps Logistics Base, Albany State University, and the county's growing medical community.

"In the beginning the founding fathers were business and community leaders who all had the same goal for Dougherty County," Barrett says. "They wanted Dougherty County to grow and be successful."

It's that tradition of excellence Barrett says he and the county's other leaders are trying to emulate.

"When I look around and see how far Dougherty County has come over the last 40 years, it makes me feel good about the community I've lived in all my life," he says. "I think we can achieve greatness, or we can fall on our face." ❧

NationsBank

$\mathscr{I}$t was no doubt a peculiar sight when James K. Vardaman and Hoyt D. Edge appeared on the streets of Albany in 1959 riding in a surrey decorated with a sign that proclaimed "Just Married." But it was the "marriage" of The Bank of Albany and Citizens and Southern Bank that was celebrated that day in 1959. And now nearly 40 years later, that partnership proved to be the foundation for what would become the city's oldest and largest bank, which became NationsBank in 1992.

C & S can trace roots in Albany back to 1929, when it purchased the combined operations of the Albany National Bank and the Exchange Bank of Albany. Sixteen years later, in 1959, with Edge serving as president, C & S bought out the Bank of Albany and increased the bank's total deposits to nearly $30 million, making it the largest bank in the city. By the year-end 1992, when Albany President Fred Hancock retired, the bank had assets of more than $169 million.

NationsBank has always been on the leading edge of technology. Although today the bank still places great value on the traditional interaction between the bank teller and the customer, the advancement of teller machines, banking over the Internet, and telephone banking allows NationsBank customers to do their banking from almost anywhere.

NationsBank has historically been a strong supporter of the Albany community. From the beginning, NationsBank of Albany had been recognized for its involvement. During Hoyt Edge's presidency, the bank was recognized statewide for its employees' participation in civic affairs. According to current Albany President Patsy Martin, each of the bank's 20 officers is involved with at least two civic organizations, meaning at any given time, 40 different community organizations are impacted by NationsBank. Ms. Martin, herself, a past Albany Woman of the Year, has served as past president of the Albany-Dougherty Chamber of Commerce and was recognized by the Georgia Economic Developer's Association as a past Economic Development Volunteer of the Year award winner.

More recently, NationsBank opened its first In-School Banking Center at Jackson Heights Elementary School. With this program, school children improve their math skills by operating their own banking center.

It is clear that NationsBank and Albany will continue their "love affair" as the bank, soon to be the leading bank in the United States, continues to provide new banking opportunities for years to come. ❧

Engineering and Equipment

A. C. Knight Sr. was a contractor at heart. But in 1937, Knight decided to open his own wholesale supply house that catered to plumbers and builders.

In partnership with John Edmondson, Knight opened Engineering and Equipment at the corner of Flint Avenue and Monroe Street in February 1937 with a store area of less than 2,000 square feet. According to third generation company President Collins Knight, his grandfather gave Edmondson 50

percent of the wholesale business and control of the day-to-day operations.

"My grandfather stayed in the contracting business," Collins said. "His true love was contracting."

Collins and his brothers John and Sanford today own E&E.

In 1955, E&E opened its current headquarters on Washington Street, with 7,000 square feet of office and showroom space and a 45,000-square-foot warehouse.

E&E handles residential and commercial plumbing, heating and air-conditioning equipment, irrigation equipment, commercial ice machines, municipal waterworks supplies, hydronics, water conditioning equipment, and industrial supplies and equipment, according to Collins. The company operates branch offices in Waycross, Columbus, Tallahassee, Panama City, and a wholly owned subsidiary operation, Georgia Industrial Supply Division, in Albany.

"Our business is tied directly to growth in residential and commercial construction," Collins said. "The success of our business is a good indicator of how a trade area is actually growing."

With 100 employees and an annual payroll of $3 million, one of the defining characteristics of E&E is its willingness to challenge itself, to "keep raising the

bar on ourselves," as Collins says, "to be even better than we were, to always strive for new levels of service and quality." In 1998, that attitude saw the company reaching significant milestones, and putting plans in motion for still more improvements.

The way Collins sees it, the plumbing distribution industry has an identity problem. "In the communities we serve, we have to be sure we aren't the best kept secret. We provide comfort of life, and we try to spend each working day pursuing a mission of raising the level of gracious living for people over a wide range of income."

"Plumbing was archaic for so long, but in the '90s, new products brought opportunities for customers to upgrade. Now the homeowner is becoming more involved in the buying decision, and becoming a more important customer," he continues.

These consumers demand information and attractive visuals and touchables, along with convenience. To deliver, E&E offers an extensive inventory, and upscale showrooms at each of its six locations, while providing ongoing educational programs for its employees.

Steady employment is another hallmark that sets E&E apart. Several of E&E's retired employees are still retained by the company on a part-time basis, including A.C. Knight Jr., past president and father of the current generation of Knight brothers until his death in 1997.

"We have a number of tenured employees who've spent a long time here and have great product knowledge and established customer relations that are of great value to us," Collins says.

Continuing the tradition of excellence established by their grandfather and father, the Knight brothers carry on many of the policies A.C. Knight Sr. and Jr. established.

One example is the company's encouragement of community involvement by its employees.

"We want employees to take an active interest in the betterment of their community," Collins says.

Officers and employees at E&E serve on many civic and charitable boards, including the United Way, the American Cancer Society, the YMCA, the Heart Association, and the Rotary, Exchange, and Kiwanis Clubs. E&E and its employees have indeed been an integral part of Albany's history and will be proud to participate in Albany's successful future.

Marbury Engineering Co.

Office of Marbury Engineering today.

R. M. Marbury Sr. was a man who thought far beyond the present. Not only was he successful in subdivision and storm water design, but he also took an active part in enhancing the natural beauty of Albany. Through his forethought and vision, oak trees were planted along both sides of Second and Third Avenues, which, on maturing, have provided a beautiful canopy to be enjoyed by generations of Albanians. Today, because of Marbury's vision, this area is one of the most picturesque in Albany.

Marbury Engineering Co. has been helping to improve the quality of life around Albany since 1913. At that time the company was known as Edgerly & Wright. In 1935 R. M. Marbury Sr., who was in business with Edgerly & Wright, took over the company, which then became Marbury Engineering Co. He, in turn, employed his son, R. M. Marbury Jr. There was a period of time between 1956 and 1962 when three generations of Marburys (each of whom was a registered engineer and surveyor) were all in the business together. Today, R. M. Marbury IV is also part of the company.

As a family of engineers and surveyors, the Marburys have been a part of most of the development of Albany, including the James H. Gray Civic Center, Darton College, the Albany Mall, Lake Loretta, and Chehaw Park, among other developments. The original surveys for the City of Albany were done by the Marburys, the main downtown surveys being done by R. M. Marbury Sr.

Subdivisions designed by Marbury Engineering include Rawson Circle, Radium Springs, Merry Acres, Sherwood Acres, Lake Park, Hidden Lakes, and Callaway Lakes.

In addition to their residential and commercial design, Marbury Engineering has also designed several golf courses. These include Grand Island Golf Course in Lee County, Pine Hills Country Club in Cordele, and the Lake Blackshear Golf Course.

The engineering business has provided much more than a good income for the Marburys and their staff. It has been a source of personal satisfaction and enjoyment. They enjoy what they do and they do it because it's fun.

The Marburys have always been active in community affairs in addition to their business and professional endeavors. R. M. Marbury Sr. served for many years as a member of the Water, Gas, & Light Commission. R. M. Marbury Jr. was the first chairman of the Albany-Dougherty County Planning Commission. R. M. Marbury III has served on the Boy Scout Executive Board and the City of Albany Tree Committee. R. M. Marbury IV is an Eagle Scout and, like his father and grandfather, is a member of Rotary International.

Marbury Engineering Co. has been a part of the growth of Albany since its earliest days. The company has helped the City to grow and progress, a legacy of which company President Ritchey M. Marbury III is proud.

The Marburys hope that they have been instrumental in improving the quality of life for this community. They love Albany, and their work is their way of helping Albany continue to be the "Good Life City." ❧

Office of Marbury Engineering in the early 1940s—it was also used as a pecan warehouse.

Albany State University

The Albany State University Academic, Administration, and International Trade Center Building; completed in March 1998.

Joseph Winthrop Holley founded the Albany Bible and Manual Training Institute in 1903 to provide religious and manual training for African-American youths of Southwest Georgia. From that day to this, the institution has been a catalyst for change throughout the region. Today it is designated as a university, but its mission to open young minds and create opportunity has remained.

The institution became a state-supported, two-year college in 1917 and was named Georgia Normal and Agricultural College. Its primary focus was agriculture although it was a highly respected source for elementary school teachers. The institution became part of the newly formed University System of Georgia in 1932. In 1943 the college was granted four-year status and authorized to confer the bachelor's degree in elementary education and home economics. This expanded focus necessitated a name change to Albany State College. Six years later the college added arts and sciences programs.

In 1954 academic offerings were expanded to include science, health and physical education, business, music, and mathematics. A four-year nursing degree was added in 1961. In the fall of 1972, a cooperative graduate program with Georgia State University was added to the curriculum.

In September, 1981, the college began offering a graduate program designed and delivered solely by its own faculty and staff.

The college was granted university status and the name of the institution changed to Albany State University in July 1996.

Today, the university has a very diverse student body and offers over 40 undergraduate and 15 graduate degrees. Under the direction of Dr. Portia Holmes Shields, Albany State University continues to educate students to become outstanding contributors to society. ❧

Georgia Power

Georgia Power's vision for the future is rooted in the proud traditions of its past.

The Georgia Power story began more than a century ago on December 3, 1883, when Georgia Electric Light Co. of Atlanta received a franchise to provide "electric lights for stores, dwellings, machine shops, depots . . . or to introduce said lights wherever desired." The company purchased its first electric light plant in 1884.

Today, the company's assets include 19 hydroelectric generating plants, 12 fossil fuel plants, two nuclear plants, and 12 gas and oil combustion turbine plants.

In 1921, Georgia Power Co. began operating a hydroelectric generating plant in Albany on the Flint River.

Shortly after the turn of the century, the hydroelectric potential of the Flint River was realized in Dougherty County.

The Albany Power & Manufacturing Co. began developing a hydroelectric plant on Muckafoonee Creek. After completion of this plant, the Alabama Power and Manufacturing Co. began acquiring nearby properties on the Flint River in anticipation of developing additional hydroelectric facilities, including the Flint River Project.

Construction of the Flint River Project began late

in 1919, and in 1921 the project was placed into operation with its first two units.

Today total GPC KW capacity at the Flint River plant is 5,400.

Serving retail and wholesale customers, Georgia Power provides electric energy to more than 1,600 communities and more than 80 percent of the state's businesses.

By providing reasonably priced, readily available electricity, the company has helped fuel the state's economic growth and prosperity, while offering sound energy solutions to Georgia's businesses.

True to their motto, "A Citizen Wherever We Serve," Georgia Power is a powerhouse of involvement, a positive force from one end of the state to the other. ❧

Alcon Associates

*I*n 1946, four construction professionals, S.J. Curry, E.G. Hightower, C.D. McKnight, and J.E. Tappan, started a new company in Albany, S.J. Curry and Co. They had worked together across the country during World War II for Algernon Blair Construction.

A year after its establishment, S.J. Curry and Co. began making a name for itself by constructing its first hospital—Patterson Hospital in Cuthbert, which recently celebrated its 50th anniversary.

In 1949 and 1950, the company successfully met the challenge of constructing its first pump station and wastewater treatment plant. Also in 1950, the company won one of 10 initial contracts awarded by the newly formed University Systems Building Authority to construct a men's dormitory at Albany State College, beginning a long-term relationship with the building authority that continues today.

In 1972, after the death of S.J. Curry and the retirement of two of the four original partners, S.J. Curry and Co. changed its name to Alcon Associates Inc. C.D. McKnight, the only remaining partner, stayed on as Alcon's Chairman of the Board of Directors.

As Alcon Associates Inc., the firm maintained the reputation and tradition of excellence established by S.J. Curry and Co. In 1983, the company completed its first construction management project, the $12-million, 155,000-square-foot Albany Civic Center.

In 1991 Alcon was selected as construction manager for the expansion program at Phoebe Putney Memorial Hospital. Alcon has successfully completed more than $100-million worth of different construction management projects at Phoebe on time and in budget.

But perhaps the company's biggest claim to building fame in Albany was its $100-million plus restoration and expansion of Albany State University.

On July 7, 1994, Albany was hit by the worst flood in the history of Georgia. On July 8, 1994, the State Board of Regents asked Alcon Associates to serve as construction manager for the flood restoration work on all 31 buildings at ASU. Just 70 days after the worst natural disaster in the state's history, ASU was ready for classes to begin.

For its outstanding effort at the ASU campus, Alcon received the Build Georgia Award and national recognition with a Build America Award.

Throughout its history, Alcon Associates has always been willing to undertake difficult projects and complete them to the total satisfaction of the owners. The staff at Alcon is committed to making each Alcon project a success and one of which its owners and designers can be proud. ❧

Interstate/Johnson Lane

*I*n 1958, Jack Dempsey was in the insurance business, but he really wanted to expand his business ventures and do something different. So Dempsey, along with his wife, Elsie, opened an office of an Atlanta stock brokerage firm in Albany.

The firm, French & Crawford Inc., opened up shop on Court Ave. Originally established to sell bonds, the Dempseys eventually began selling stocks. Today, the company is a full-service brokerage firm.

In 1962 the firm merged with Johnson, Lane, Space, Smith and Co. in Savannah. The new brokerage house soon outgrew the small office on Court Avenue and moved its operations to the former Firehouse Saloon building on Pine Avenue, across from the courthouse. Ironically, in 1985, the office was destroyed by fire, and the firm relocated to its present site on Dawson Road.

In 1988, Johnson, Lane, Space, Smith and Co. was acquired by Interstate Securities in Charlotte, N.C. The new name for the combined companies became Interstate/Johnson Lane, a public company traded on the New York Stock Exchange under the symbol IJL.

Since 1993, the office has been managed by Ben Benford, first vice president, along with Randy

Alford, vice president, and Michael Cohen, financial consultant. Sabrina Denmark and Tina Kozuch serve as assistants in the office. ❧

YMCA of Albany

"He who builds a building to build people builds for eternity." Inspired by these words, 100 businessmen met on October 25, 1909, at the New Albany Hotel for a purpose: to establish and build a YMCA in Albany. The worldwide movement was then 65 years old, and local leaders recognized that such an organization was needed in Albany. Led by Judge F.F. Putney, the initial campaign was successful and raised $30,000 in five days. These funds provided for a Pine and Jefferson Avenue facility, the YMCA's home for over fifty years. In 1963 Albany leaders came together to build the current central facility at 1701 Gillionville Road. Today, this site anchors the YMCA's five-county operation, which includes a 50-acre Sports Park with outdoor aquatics center, soccer fields, gymnastics center, basketball pavilion, and day camp. Programs range from child care, youth sports, and gymnastics to wellness education, adult fitness, aquatics, and older adult activities. And while specific programs and facilities have changed with the needs of the community, the YMCA has continued to place emphasis on character development. It is through the strengthening of values that YMCA volunteers, staff, and members accomplish the mission of putting Christian principles into practice through programs that build a healthy spirit, mind, and body for all. 🙢

Dougherty County School System

The Dougherty County School System can trace its roots to 1885, when the desire for public education in Albany resulted in a campaign to raise $5,000 for a school building. A lot was purchased on the northwest corner of Flint Avenue and Madison Street. On this site, the two-story Albany Academy was constructed. The school opened in the fall of 1886.

By 1905 a demand had grown for a city system of public schools. The next year a special act of the Legislature established a city school system. S.R. deJarnette was elected its first superintendent.

In 1951 the city school system and the county school system were merged through a legislative act to form the Dougherty County School System. This act specified that the Board of Education should consist of seven members, county residents, for at least four years. The City Commissioners, the County Commissioners, and the Grand Jury appointed two members each. The six appointed elected the seventh member by majority vote. Since 1988 the seven members of the Board have been elected by the people.

Today, the school system is one of the largest in the state, operating 15 elementary schools, 6 middle schools, and 4 high schools. Its stated mission is "in cooperation with parents and community, to provide all students with the skills, knowledge, and attitudes necessary to be responsible, productive citizens."

Under current superintendent Dr. John W. Culbreath, the system is driven by the belief that "All Children Can Learn, and Together We Can Make It Happen." The system exemplifies dedication to quality by embracing innovation while still providing a strong foundation in the basics. The system, known as *A System That Cares*, prides itself on interaction with business and industry, with government and service agencies, and, most of all, with the home. 🙢

CHAPTER VII

WORLD WAR II TO 1969

Decades of Challenge and Growth

The 1952 Armed Forces Day Parade moving east on Broad. Palm trees along the main streets gave the city a distinctive appearance. Locals recall the 1950s as the heyday of downtown Albany.

WALB-TV

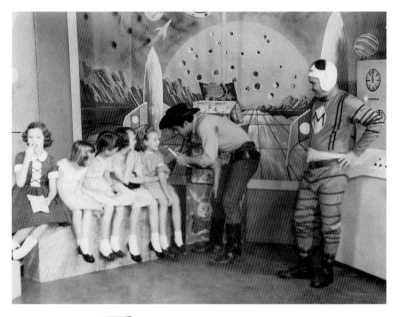

The Captain Mercury Show with host Grady Shadburn and TV star Robert Fuller from Laramie.

For 47 years Albany has been home to WALB-TV, Channel 10, the NBC affiliate for south Georgia. In 1957 WALB became an NBC affiliate and remained the only station licensed in the Albany market until 1982. WALB-TV was founded by James H. Gray Sr., one of Albany's most influential citizens and mayors.

As the dominant television station in the market, WALB has been second only once, when it was the second TV station to go on the air in the state of Georgia in 1954. WALB has been number one ever since.

Due to its focus on local news, popular programming, state-of-the-art technology, and solid management of costs and resources, WALB-TV has built a solid reputation as an active, responsible, and reliable member of the Albany business community.

A testament to the station's pioneering ways is a color studio camera—one of the first made by RCA—that was once used at WALB, but is now housed at the Smithsonian Museum in Washington, D.C., in the Science & Technology Building.

"That camera was originally purchased to tape a First Baptist Church program, which had been filmed in black and white," station General Manager Jim Wilcox says. "Local programming was very big in the early days because there were so few networks and a shortage of network programming."

"Those gaps in network programming meant the station had to come up with local programming content of its own," Wilcox says. In the late 1950s, early 1960s, the *The Captain Mercury Show* went on the air, a favorite of Albany residents.

"A lot of Albany residents' fondest memories are of *The Captain Mercury Show*," Wilcox says. "Members of the *Captain Mercury* studio audience are

The first color studio camera made by RCA. This TK 41 is displayed in Washington D.C. in the Science and Technology building at the Smithsonian Museum.

today presidents of some of Albany's largest companies."

That tradition of live local programming continues today at WALB in two daily live programs that have become a part of south Georgia life: *Today In Georgia*, Sunday through Saturday, 6-7 a.m., and *Town & Country*, Monday through Friday, noon-12:30 p.m. Both shows feature guests from all over the region, discussing topics important to everyday life, from business, agriculture, and charity work to fashion, cooking, and medical advice.

"These shows are remnants of what was popular when TV began—live local programming," Wilcox says. "That tradition remains popular here today, versus the trend of flashy talk shows."

The *Today In Georgia* show is America's number one program in audience domination, with an amazing 99 percent in-market share of viewing as reported by the Nielsen Ratings Service. Due to its popularity, in January, 1997, WALB expanded the show to seven mornings per week.

The *Town & Country* program often leaves the studio and travels live to at least 20 area towns in the Albany area as part of a promotion called "My Home Town." These special on-location events celebrate the annual festivals which make our communities unique and provide important tourism dollars.

In 1992, the station took local programming a step further and created *Dialogue*, a show devoted solely to addressing minority issues.

"When we started the show six years ago, there wasn't a program in south Georgia like it that addressed minority issues," Wilcox says. "I think it's a misconception that the news reporting in the market is not fair and balanced, but the perception exists."

"The purpose this program serves is it emphasizes the need for information about the minority community." The program was started in conjunction with

the Coalition for Diversity and The Criterion Club.

Newscenter 10 is the flagship of WALB-TV's public service. Channel 10 delivers up-to-date news, sports, and weather information three and one-half hours each day, Monday through Friday, and two hours on Saturday and Sunday. Newscenter 10 is the most popular newscast in more than 40 counties surrounding Albany. Additional features of interest such as "Healthbeat," "Monday Talks," "Instant Car Clinic," "The Stock Report," and "The Locker Room Report" are area favorites.

Throughout its history WALB has demonstrated a commitment to community service. In an average year, WALB produces three local live telethons: The Children's Miracle Network, Easter Seals, and "Let's Make a Bid to Benefit the Albany Museum." Additionally, WALB will produce public service announcements for at least 65 organizations, three major campaign presentation tapes, live hour and half-hour programs from nine locations, and news coverage of literally hundreds of civic events and nonprofit organizations.

In recent years, WALB has been tested not only by the challenges of advancing technology, but also by Mother Nature herself. In both cases, the station has overcome the odds and served its community.

In 1993 WALB began plans for the first statewide live sporting event originating from Albany. The 4th Annual KFC High School Basketball Classic was held at the Albany Civic Center and was fed via satellite to 12 TV stations across Georgia, Florida, and Alabama. Because of the interest in outstanding players from their region, a station in Las Vegas and Cincinnati also carried Albany's broadcast.

In July, 1994, the services of WALB-TV and Newscenter 10 were severely tested during the great Flood of '94. WALB stayed on the air literally nonstop to get vital information out to those affected by this terrible tragedy.

Later that year, WALB again took the lead in the state and hosted a debate in a hot gubernatorial race, Gov. Zell Miller vs. Guy Milner. Albany fed the rest of the state this debate via satellite. In 1996 WALB-TV repeated this public service by hosting a statewide senatorial debate, Guy Milner vs. Max Cleland.

In January, 1997, WALB-TV began five-minute news broadcasts 40 times per day in cooperation with

TCI cable company on the CNN Headline News channel. In June, WALB rolled out a full-blown Web page project with up-to-the-minute news, sports, and weather information, including photographs.

And WALB's efforts have not gone unnoticed.

In 1993 the Georgia Association of Broadcasters named WALB as the "Station of the Year." Adding to that are awards for the "Community Service Station of the Year," "Agriculture Promotion of the Year," and the "Promotion of the Year."

The following year, WALB received national recognition as the first commercial TV station to air a 30-part, half-hour series, *Learn to Read on TV*, designed to teach adults to read. The effort earned the top award from The National Association of Broadcasters and Georgia Partners in Education.

In 1997 the station won "Best Newscast" in the state of Georgia, presented by the Georgia Association of Broadcasters, for its 6 o'clock show—a first for the station.

When he looks to the future, Wilcox comes back to WALB's commitment to community service.

"I think the reasons WALB will continue to dominate the market are our concern for providing local news, sports, and weather and our concentration on giving the community what it wants and what it needs." ❧

Jim Wallace, Dawn Hobby, Joe Coffey, Yolanda Amadeo.

Jim Wilcox
President/General Manager of WALB-TV

Merck & Co.

Scene at ground-breaking for the Flint River Plant in Albany, Georgia on May 2, 1952. H.N. Fiaccone and James J. Kerrigan.

*I*n the 1940s, Merck & Co. was facing a competitive challenge. Other pharmaceutical companies that had previously bought Merck chemicals began making their own. That led Chairman George W. Merck and President James J. Kerrigan to make two important strategic choices—both of which are still benefiting Albany today.

The first decision was to move into pharmaceuticals, a decision that led to the 1953 merger with Sharp & Dohme; and to broaden the company's manufacturing base with a new plant in Georgia.

In the early 1950s, after touring much of the South, "Joe" Fiaccone and D. H. McCondichie picked Albany for Merck's new plant. Situated on the Flint River, the 704-acre site had an ample water supply, several rail connections, and a good workforce.

By the time Merck merged with Sharp & Dohme, the Flint River Plant was ready to begin production. The Flint River Plant manufactures bulk active ingredients for many of the corporation's top pharmaceuticals.

Flint River's first product was a new anti-infective, sulfanilamide. Before the sulfa drugs were discovered in the 1930s, doctors had been unable to deal effectively with infections. With the discovery of the sulfa drugs, however, doctors used sulfanilamide to treat bacterial infections in both humans and animals.

As Merck entered a period of vigorous expansion at home and abroad, the Flint River Plant developed new facilities to manufacture the innovative products coming out of Merck's labs. In the 1960s Flint River built a second factory to produce the breakthrough antihypertensive alpha-methyldopa (Aldomet). Flint River also produced the diuretic chlorothiazide (Diuril) and hydrochlorothiazide (Hydrodiuril), as well as probenecid (Benemid) for treating gout.

In 1976 the plant introduced a new style of modular factory, designed to manufacture a variety of products as demands shifted. The plan was excellent, but the first product the new Factory 3 made was in such demand that Flint River just continued making cefoxitin (Mefoxin), one of Merck's successful antibiotics. In the late 1970s this computer-controlled facility was one of two cutting edge chemical manufacturing plants for Merck in the U.S.

Today, there are three working factories, a power plant, waste treatment facilities, incinerators, and several other manufacturing and support storage areas.

Throughout the 1980s and '90s Flint River has continued to demonstrate its ability to keep pace with Merck's rapid growth. New, state-of-the-art process control technology was installed in one factory; and well-designed, flexible process manifold systems were

Groundbreaking for the Flint River Plant on May 2, 1952.

installed in a second modular factory. These two systems have given the plant the flexibility to manufacture omeprazole (Prilosec), a gastrointestinal drug for the treatment of ulcers, and simvastatin (Zocor), a cholesterol-lowering drug.

Flint River also produces the active ingredient for market newcomers Cozaar and Hyzaar, hypertensive drugs; and Crixivan, a protease inhibitor used in the treatment of HIV/AIDS. Today, the Flint River Plant is an integral part of Merck's Manufacturing Division, producing several of Merck's newest growth products, in addition to the more mature medications.

In 1997 the plant was undergoing its fourth phase of expansion in the past three years, running parallel with dynamic corporate growth. That expansion was valued at $75 million.

Increased demand for both new and existing drugs is propelling the expansions at the Flint River Plant. Merck has introduced eight new products since 1995, and at least eight more new drugs are on-line for regulatory clearance in 1998.

How quickly a plant's capacity can be expanded to manufacture a drug and how fast a new drug can get to the patient dictates selection for expansion sites. In the case of Flint River, its track record shows the plant is highly capable of rapid conversions with low capital costs.

"Our portfolio of products is strong," Plant Manager Tony Musiol says. "We had the flexibility and adaptability to handle the expansion for new products and maintain and increase the volume of production of existing drugs."

The local expansions and corporate strength also bode well for Albany and the local economy.

The workforce, at 300 when the expansions started, totaled 559 employees at the end of 1997. In 1996, the Flint River Plant's payroll was more than $38 million. Another $20 million was spent in local purchases and $5 million in utilities.

"Being a good corporate neighbor is more than economic impact," Musiol says. "Our employees are involved throughout the community, and we're committed to a clean environment, which impacts the quality of life for the entire community."

On-site wastewater treatment facilities at the Flint River Plant have doubled capacity, and emissions have dropped 97 percent since 1987.

*Factory 1,
December, 1952.*

In fact, Merck's efforts in protecting the environment have earned the company several prestigious awards both nationally and regionally, including the Award for Achievement in Air Quality from the Georgia Chapter of the Air and Waste Management Association for 1997, 1996, and 1993. In 1997, the Flint River Plant also received the Outstanding Pollution Prevention Practice Award from this organization.

Other recognitions for the company include the Governor's Award for Existing Industry from The Georgia Economic Development Commission for outstanding economic and social contributions; and the Flint River Plant was named the 1997 Industry of the Year by the Albany chapter of the NAACP.

The plant's history is a case study in how productivity can be blended with safety and with sophisticated, high-quality products.

As Flint River stands poised for the next century, today's Albany employees are aiming to make its future as productive as its past.

"We're immensely proud of what the Flint River group has been able to do," Musiol says. "We've shown this plant has unparalleled value in the corporate overview. No matter the challenge, Flint River was always the option that met the timing, and that's good news for everyone." ❧

Deerfield-Windsor School

eerfield School had a mere 15 students and two teachers when it opened in 1964 at Westview Baptist Church—the vision of a group of Albany business and professional men interested in a quality education for their children.

With 34 years and a merger with Windsor Park Academy behind it, Deerfield-Windsor School boasted in 1997 a record enrollment of more than 770 students spread over two campuses, 100 percent college placement for its students, and an average score of 1153 on the Scholastic Assessment Test (SAT).

"We are proud of the fact that 100 percent of our graduates go to college," Headmaster W.T. Henry says. "We have a very strong college preparatory curriculum and an outstanding faculty and staff at Deerfield-Windsor."

Deerfield-Windsor was founded under the corporate charter "United Parents, Incorporated" as an independent, college preparatory school in September 1964. W.T. Bodenhammer, a former member of the Georgia Board of Education and a 26-year veteran of the educational system, was one of the original petitioners and would become the school's first principal.

In 1966, 232 children enrolled at Deerfield, and an architect was employed to build a campus on nine acres of donated land on Stuart Avenue in northwest Albany. When it was complete, the school boasted 14

Middle/upper school on Stuart Avenue.

classrooms and a library for its 232 students and 12 teachers by the fall of 1966.

Governed by a Board of Trustees, the school's first chairman of the board was Spec Dozier, who oversaw what would be the first of several expansion programs.

In 1968 an additional 10 classrooms, cafeteria, and gym were constructed. Again, in 1970, the school was enlarged by nine more classrooms, a band room, and additional dressing rooms. The lower school was renovated in 1992, and a new computer lab was established. A new cafeteria was constructed at the middle/upper school in 1995. During the 1996-1997 school year a new gym capable of seating 1,100 people was completed in time for Deerfield-Windsor to host the Region 3AAA basketball tournament.

The middle/upper school campus on Stuart Avenue houses grades 6-12, while students in pre-K through fifth grade attend the lower school campus on Beattie Road.

During the 1997-1998 school year, the Deerfield-Windsor Knights were the Georgia Independent School Association state champions in girls tennis, boys tennis, and baseball. They were Region 3AAA champions in boys basketball, boys and girls tennis, and baseball. The math and Scholathon teams were victorious, and the literary team won first place in the state.

Headmaster Henry, who has directed the school since 1989, says he is confident of the bright future of Deerfield-Windsor.

"Deerfield-Windsor School is the finest college preparatory school in south Georgia," he says. "The success of our alumni in a broad range of career paths clearly attests to the value of a Deerfield-Windsor education. Each graduating class seems to surpass the previous one with impressive college admission statistics. This is a school of which we can all be proud." ❧

Lower school on Beattie Road.

Albany Technical Institute

From its humble beginnings in 1961 to today, Albany Technical Institute has evolved to meet the ever-changing needs of the business and industrial communities of southwest Georgia, expanding its campus and its course offerings as employers' needs in the region have changed.

On July 14, 1958, the Georgia Legislature approved the construction of 26 area vocational-technical schools throughout the state. Albanians were the first to voice their approval, and in 1959 construction began on the first building on Lippett Drive. Two years later the $325,000 Monroe Area Vocational-Technical School, initiated under the Dougherty Board of Education, opened its doors for registration of 175 students.

students are enrolled each quarter in certificate programs, seminars, teleconferences, and customized training offered through Continuous Career Learning and Business and Industry Services.

As home to plants of some of the largest manufacturers in the world, Albany and Dougherty County have unique needs in terms of a skilled labor pool. In order to meet those needs, a team comprised of 11 local industry plant managers and Albany Tech leaders came together in October of 1990 to discuss new methods to meet local industries' employment and training requirements. The result was the Technology Training Center that prepares students to operate, to troubleshoot, and to manage the complex, highly automated and computerized manufacturing process operations of today and in the 21st century.

The Technology Training Center opened in 1995. It is a $3-million, 20,000-square-foot building housing the Regional Quick Start Center for southwest Georgia, a one-of-a-kind 85-ton automated manufacturing line plus an instrumentation and process simulator controlled with a Honeywell TDC-3000 computer system.

First of seven Albany Technical Institute buildings. Built in 1962.

The state and county boards soon established the separate Albany Area Vocational-Technical School on the corner of South Slappey Boulevard and Lowe Road. The $400,000 facility opened with 12 programs in 1962.

Ten years later, the two units were merged in a new 78,169-square-foot, $1.4-million facility on Lowe Road. Additional programs were offered and the existing programs were expanded.

In response to Albany's growing health care community, in 1980, construction was completed on a 60,000-square-foot facility at a cost of $1.2 million, adding Health Care Technology and five other programs.

Seventh building on campus. George M. Kirkland, Jr. Building houses a conference center, administrative offices and student services.

On July 1, 1988, Albany Area Vocational-Technical School became a unit of the Georgia Department of Technical and Adult Education. A local board of directors was established, and the name was changed to Albany Technical Institute.

Albany Tech has experienced phenomenal growth since its inception, with approximately 2,000 students enrolled in credit programs today. Approximately 2,500 additional

"Albany Technical Institute will be known as the flagship technical institute in the Southeastern United States," says Albany Tech President Dr. Anthony Parker. "It will be recognized for its excellent record of student achievement, services to business and industry, state-of-the-art technology educational facilities, excellent faculty and staff, the delivery of quality educational and student programming, and as the most attractive place of employment in technical postsecondary education."

Mathews Oaklawn Chapel

Growing up in Montezuma, Georgia, Gary Mathews and his brother Mike Mathews spent many a day cutting the grass and digging graves by hand at their father's funeral home and cemetery.

Mathews Oaklawn Chapel Funeral Home was started in 1949 on N. Jefferson Street as the Woodall Funeral Home. For 35 years, the funeral business was housed in one of Albany's oldest houses, Dr. W. L. Davis's house, which was built in 1876 by Confederate Col. Edwin Wight.

When the brothers came to Albany in 1976, Mike was 23 and Gary was 20. They were cutting the grass in front of their own funeral home when a potential customer walked up and asked to see the funeral director. "That's us," the young brothers replied. While the customer at first may have been put off by the brothers' young age, it wasn't long before their lifetime of knowledge of the funeral business shone through.

"We were raised in it," Gary Mathews says. "We know the business."

The brothers also knew at a very early age they would follow in their father's footsteps, Walter M. Mathews Jr., but it wouldn't be in Montezuma. Instead, the pair headed south 60 miles to Albany.

Mathews Oaklawn Chapel Funeral Home was started in 1949 on N. Jefferson Street as the Woodall Funeral Home. Gary and Mike, along with their father, acquired the business in 1976.

For 35 years, the funeral business was housed in one of Albany's oldest houses, Dr. W. L. Davis's house, which was built in

In 1984, a new location on Gillionville Road was built to better serve the public in a quieter location.

1876 by Confederate Col. Edwin Wight.

The Wight-Davis house was one of the residential showplaces of Albany. Originally five stories, the home was one of the first in Albany with lights and a telephone.

As the business grew, the brothers saw a need for a new facility to better serve the public in a quieter atmosphere. So in 1984, a new location at 3206 Gillionville Road was built, where the funeral home still operates today.

Starting out, the Mathews offered just basic funeral services, but today they offer the full range of funeral services, including monuments and cremations, and in 1997, the brothers bought a cemetery in Leesburg.

"As we saw the growth in Lee County, we saw the need for an upgraded cemetery and facility," Gary says. "So on the 100th anniversary of the Leesburg Cemetery in 1997, we entered into a joint project with the City of Leesburg."

There were no more lots available in the city cemetery, where many of Leesburg's leading citizens are buried. The city still owns a small part of the cemetery, but the Mathews purchased an adjoining 30 acres around the city cemetery to create Leesburg Cemetery Inc.

"We're continuing to upgrade the grounds," Gary says. "Since we purchased the property, we've installed new wrought iron gates, brick entrances, shrubbery, and irrigation. Expansions and upgrades at the cemetery will continue."

The Mathews also established a trust fund last year that will serve to maintain the cemetery and grounds, Gary says.

The Mathews brothers are proud of their funeral home and are committed to providing quality, compassionate funeral services in the Albany area.

"It's rewarding to us to be able to help families and serve them in their time of need," Gary says. "Our motto is personal, courteous service." ❧

Doublegate Country Club, LTD

*A*ngus and Ava Alberson acquired 1,000 acres of pristine Georgia land in the early 1950s. They and their two children, Jenny and Mike, enjoyed the land for almost ten years. They often went on jeep and horseback riding outings, hunting for game, or picnicking at the Blue Hole. During those happy, peaceful years, they called the homeplace and land "Westerly Plantation." It wasn't long before it occurred to them, that the beautiful place might be enjoyed by many others.

In 1960 they decided to build a gathering place for friends and family that would eventually become known as the Doublegate Country Club. Mr. Alberson set aside 202 acres for golf, tennis, swimming and social purposes. The Alberson family toured the finest golf courses from Miami to the great Carolina courses in Hilton Head and Pinehurst, on up to Washington, D.C. When the tour was finished, the family decided to retain George W. Cobb of Greenville, South Carolina, to design the golf course at Doublegate. The Alberson land and street planners and the late Gene Martini and his associates, now called Baldwin Associates, designed South Doublegate and St. Andrews together as a single development.

Much thought was given to every design aspect of Doublegate. Mr. Alberson erected scaffolds so he could better decide on a location for the clubhouse that would present the most breathtaking view. The first plan of the Club building was largely inspired by Arnold Palmer's Country Club of Miami where the entryway is between two floors. The mound at the front door makes the Club entrance the highest point in Dougherty County. Richard V. Richards was the architect who gathered the multitude of inspirations and adapted them for use in the Clubhouse. The engineer for the construction was Mr. John Sperry and the Clubhouse was built by Oxford Construction.

The lockers were inspired by the Doral Country Club in Miami while the entrance gate columns are exact duplicates of those at the once famous, but since razed, Roney Plaza Hotel in Miami. The golf course opened for play on Thursday, August 6, 1964. Later, Mr. Alberson's interest was purchased by Mr. O.D. Carlton and Mr. C.T. Oxford (leading and defining forces behind the Club).

The club continued to operate under private ownership until 1979 when it was sold to members. The golf course has undergone a multitude of improvements since its opening 29 years ago, including a Maxi irrigation system in 1988 and a greens renovation in 1992.

John LaFoy, a renown golf course architect who had previously worked with George Cobb, was hired to design new green complexes, including bunkers, mounds, etc. for each hole. Tifton Golf Services was hired as the contractor and work began in January 1992. The membership played temporary greens during the course of the renovation. The new USGA specification greens opened for play in August 1992.

Doublegate has hosted several tournaments including two Men's GSGA Amateur Championships, the Women's GSGA Championship, the State Seniors Championship, and the GSGA Men's Four Ball among others. The annual Hospice Charity Tournament remains a local favorite.

The Clubhouse is currently undergoing a major renovation that started in May of 1997. Beautiful appointments and fine amenities are maintained and added to the Club over the years, but the graceful elegance of Doublegate remains a stalwart base of the Dougherty County business and social elite. ❧

SunTrust Bank

A group of Albany businessmen knew a good opportunity when they saw one back in 1960, and with an initial offering of $1.5 million worth of stock, the group started what would become SunTrust Bank.

The First National Bank of Albany opened in August of 1960 at 316 Broad Avenue. By December of that year, the bank employed two officers and six employees. Deposits at the time were $1.3 million, while loans totaled more than $800,000 and assets of more than $2.1 million were recorded.

"At that time, there were only two other banks in Albany," original investor Harry Willson recalls. "We thought there was a need for another bank."

According to Willson, J.W. Toney, a banker out of Doerun, and Hal B. Brimberry, an Albany insurance man, originally proposed the idea to the other investors.

"J.W. Toney and his brother B.B. had a little bank down in Doerun," Willson says. "They knew a good bit about the banking business. And Hal Brimberry was an insurance man with Walden & Brimberry; they were two of the chief proponents of it."

Brimberry served as the bank's first chairman of the board, according to Willson. Other original board members included some of Albany's leading businessmen and most influential citizens at the time, including E.C. Lancaster, B.C. Gardner Jr., W.M. Hagins, J.W.

Construction of new bank at 410 W. Broad—opened May 21, 1977. Since then, two additional floors have been added.

Toney, T.B. Chandler, H.V. TenHagen, M.E. Wages, and Roy Dial.

Less than a year after its opening, First National Bank moved to 410 Broad Avenue—the address the bank still calls home today.

As the bank celebrated its 10th anniversary in 1970, assets had grown to nearly $23 million, while deposits had grown to nearly $21 million and loans had increased to more than $10 million.

"The bank made money the first year it was open and has made money ever since then," Willson says.

So it was no surprise when Trust Co. of Georgia started making overtures to the bank, Willson says, and on July 1, 1977, First National was acquired by Trust Co. of Georgia.

On Sept. 1, 1983, the name of the bank was changed to Trust Co. Bank of South Georgia.

Under the stewardship of Trust Co., the bank acquired five other southwest Georgia banks, including First National Bank of Thomasville, Farmers Bank of Pelham, the Bank of Worth County, the First Federal Savings & Loan Association, and Trust Co. Bank of Coffee County.

In October of 1995, the bank officially changed its name to SunTrust Bank, South Georgia, N.A.

Today SunTrust boasts 15 locations throughout southwest Georgia, assets of more than $669 million, deposits of more than $500 million, and a loan volume of more than $515 million.

After more than 100 years of working closely with its customers, SunTrust's service philosophy of helping customers be ready for life is much more than a promise; it's deeply ingrained in the entire organization.

Their experienced staff offers customers a full array of financial options, as well as a supportive attitude in helping them reach their financial goals. ❧

Original bank at 410 W. Broad, opened June 5, 1961.

Brad Lanier Oil Co.

At 17, Brad Lanier was already an accomplished pilot with years of flying experience.

B rad Lanier was an avid aviator. A Brigadier General in the Georgia Air National Guard, Lanier made his first solo flight when he was just 12 years old.

"We like to say he was an 'addict to the air,'" son Jeff Lanier says. "He had given some thought to flying for an airline full-time, but decided for his family he wouldn't do that."

A father of five, Lanier decided instead to go into business for himself. On April 19, 1965, Brad Lanier Oil Co. was born.

"We had no experience in the business," 33-year employee Hans Pomeroy says. "We learned something new every day."

Pomeroy now serves as president of the company, which is a wholesale supplier of petroleum, gasoline, diesel, and lubricant products. Today the company operates four retail stores in the Albany area, employs more than 60 people, and boasts a more than $1-million payroll. But it wasn't always that way, Pomeroy recalls.

Business was slim in those early days; a good day was when someone ordered a radiator cap or a fan belt.

"That first year we only netted $300," he says. "It was very tight in the beginning. Brad had to supplement his income by flying for the National Guard. That money the airline was offering looked really good compared to what we were making."

But no matter how tight things were in the beginning, Pomeroy says Lanier never talked of throwing in the towel.

And there's been no looking back. Brad Lanier Oil Co. is one of the largest independent motor fuel companies in south Georgia. In 1997 the company posted more than $50 million in sales.

In the beginning, the company was more service-station oriented, checking under the hood and making

35 years later as a retired colonel in USAF and retired brigadier general in Georgia Air National Guard. Successful father, public servant, and president/founder of Brad Lanier Oil Co., Inc.

service calls. Gradually, the company's focus shifted more to the sale of wholesale fuels, which today makes up 95 percent of the business.

"In the early days, we didn't go across the river," Pomeroy says, referring to the Flint River, which divides east and west Albany. "Now, we serve customers within a 90-mile radius."

While wholesale fuels and oil make up a majority of the company's business, retail sales represents the fastest growing segment of the operation.

"Our goal is to be the best in the business," Vice President Jeff Lanier says. "Now our company is seeing the most growth in the retail side of the business, through the convenience stores."

The company branched into the convenience store business about a decade ago, and the company now boasts two fueling stations and four stores—Homerun Foods—in Albany and Leesburg.

Though his father passed away in 1988, the younger Lanier says he thinks his dad would be proud of the success the company has achieved.

"I think he'd probably slap us on the back and say keep on going," Lanier says. "There was never a set number of stores or gallons he wanted to sell. The goal was just to continue to grow, and that's what we've done." ❧

Draffin & Tucker, LLP

*W*hen Fondren M. Draffin started his own accounting firm in Moultrie in 1948, he could never have imagined that one day it would grow into a regional firm serving clients from Georgia to Texas—but it has.

Draffin started out more or less preparing income tax returns for individuals and small businesses. In 1963, he selected his first partner, W. Hubert Tucker Jr.

In 1972, the Moultrie firm branched out and opened a satellite practice in Albany. The practice was located in a small house on North Slappey Boulevard, which still stands at the corner of Slappey and 7th Avenue today.

Larry L. Ruis was the partner from Moultrie charged with opening the Albany office, with the help of two other accountants and a secretary.

At the time, Draffin & Tucker saw great potential in the Albany market for its services; however, those expectations have been far exceeded.

Initially, the firm brought some of its clients from Moultrie to Albany, but in time, the practice merged with three smaller Albany firms to form the nucleus of what would become one of Albany's largest local accounting firms.

Today, the firm boasts 60 employees, including approximately 34 accountants and 11 partners and offers a myriad of services, including auditing, consulting, accounting services, and related tax preparation and planning.

Four principles serve as the cornerstones of professional services at Draffin & Tucker. First, the firm is dedicated to quality, as demonstrated by its continuing education requirements, the range of its expertise, and its voluntary decision to hold to the highest level of CPA standards—the Securities and Exchange Commission section requirements. Second, the accountants at Draffin & Tucker pride themselves on timely service to ensure their clients have current and accurate data in order to make informed business decisions. Third, the firm's clients are assured of personal attention from the partner, manager, and service team assigned to them, and finally, Draffin & Tucker is committed to delivering superior performance at competitive rates.

For 50 years, Draffin & Tucker has supplied a full range of professional accounting services to small businesses, large corporations, individuals, governmental entities, nonprofit agencies, and health care providers.

One of the biggest changes at the firm in the last 20 years has been its foray into the health care industry.

In 1978, Draffin & Tucker counted three hospitals and nursing homes among its clientele. Today the firm serves more than 140 hospitals, nursing homes, and other health-care related entities.

Draffin & Tucker provides auditing, Medicare/Medicaid reimbursement, and management services to health care clients in Georgia, Florida, Alabama, Texas, South Carolina, and Louisiana. The firm serves more health-care facilities than most accounting firms in the region. Their clients range in size from 21-bed hospitals to regional medical centers with more than 600 beds.

It was no accident Draffin & Tucker ended up servicing the health care industry. Early on, the firm identified the health care industry as something extraordinary. With that understanding and a lot of hard work, Draffin & Tucker was able to gain an expertise in the largest growing industry in the United States.

And it's that foresight and drive Draffin & Tucker is counting on to take it into the 21st century. ❧

For 50 years, Draffin & Tucker has supplied a full range of professional accounting services to small businesses, large corporations, individuals, governmental entities, nonprofit agencies, and health care providers.

S & S Company of Georgia, Inc.

S & S Company of Georgia, Inc., which is celebrating its 50th year in business, is a closely held family corporation and might be described as a classic example of American entrepreneurship. The Company was founded in the spring of 1948 by Ernst Skalla, a German immigrant chemist who, after having served

Randy Skalla, V.P., Mgr. of Sales & R&D; Carolyn LaSchober, Pres. & CFO; Lan Skalla, V.P. Internal Operations & Haz Mat Control with Company awards plaque

five years in the U.S. armed forces during World War II with an all-Georgia outfit under the command of the former Governor of Georgia, Marvin Griffin, landed in Albany, Georgia, as manager of a local Chicago-owned winery. He met and married Carol and a year later decided that he would like to have his own business. Ernst had a very solid background as a chemist and extensive business management experience. His unlikely partner in his planned endeavor was Carol, whose background was in theatre, dance, and acting! The third member of the team was an energetic, bright young man, Love Davis, who was hired away from Carol's father. Love stayed with the Company for 48 years until he reached retirement age. The physical location of this new operation was a closed corner in a pecan processing plant owned by Carol's father. With Ernst's background and Carol's willingness to learn, a sanitary supply business seemed a "natural," and the small distributorship was off and running. The business grew and prospered, and when Carol's father's health declined, he retired, and S & S Company occupied the entire building.

By the mid '60s, S & S had dropped most of the "name" brand products and was now compounding its own proprietary products servicing the market. In 1972, Ernst passed away and sons Lan, who was in the Air Force, and Randy, in college, came home to "help" run the business. While raising their sons, Carol had kept her hand in the business in a small way, entering the books and helping out when needed. She and her sons were determined to keep the business afloat. With the cooperation of the Company's financial institutions, accounting firm, suppliers, and customers the

Company fought its way back. Lan took on internal operations and later found his niche in Hazardous Material Control, which is now a viable part of the Company's operation. Randy was a born salesman. His expertise is to solve a client's problem by creating a customized product.

Today there are four departments in operation—Industrial Chemical, Biomedical, Hazardous Material, and the newly added Rubber Group.

An outstanding accomplishment was a certification from the State of California in August of 1994. Out of 200 technologies tested, five were chosen for certification, and S & S Company's Formalex®-FRC-3™, which neutralizes formaldehyde, was certified for the biomedical technology.

In April of 1998, the Columbia space shuttle launched carrying S & S Company's Fan Pad G.L.™ for use in the scientific tissue studies, which were conducted during the shuttle's mission. The Company is now in the process of developing a product and equipment for another scientific shuttle flight in the year 2002.

From a three-person operation in the corner of a warehouse building, adding additional land and buildings, S & S Company has evolved into a nationwide provider and international exporter with a master distributor in California and Canada and distributors in Australia and Japan. She counts among her customers many *Fortune 500* companies and hospitals across the nation. Her manufacturers' representatives cover 30 out of the 50 states—AND NOW, OUTER SPACE!!!

She is also proud that a third-generation family member joined the firm in 1997. Randy's son, Marc, is proving to be a most creditable addition to the firm.

In summary, their profile reads: "S & S Company is a technical leader in the manufacturing of environmentally safe specialty chemicals and hazardous chemical control products. Well-known in the manufacturing industry as the 'Problem Solvers,' S & S Company has created a reputation as a highly diversified, yet, very specialized chemical researcher, developer, and producer."

"S & S Company works as a cooperative partner with its customers, solving their chemical needs, no matter how varied, and in the process, reducing employee exposure and environmental impact through creative chemistry. Therefore, a safer, more productive workplace is created with fewer government regulations and less government paperwork. With each new challenge comes a new opportunity for us to not only serve a particular customer's needs but, also, many times creates an opportunity for us to serve an entire industry." S & S attributes much of her success to the capability of following the change in market demand.

The Company is now proudly looking forward to the next 50 years in business! ❧

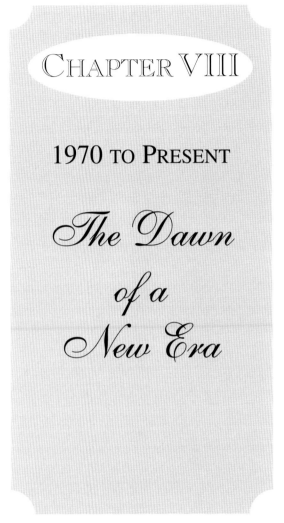

CHAPTER VIII

1970 TO PRESENT

*The Dawn
of a
New Era*

*The volunteer
response to the
1994 flood was
inspiring. Many
residents filled
sand bags for
people desperate
to save their homes
and businesses.
Photo courtesy of
U.S. Army Corps
of Engineers.*

Thronateeska Heritage Foundation Inc.

At the end of the tracks, the old train station is where Albany's history begins.

By the 1910s, Albany was the railroad hub of Southwest Georgia. Increasing traffic required more elaborate passenger facilities, and in 1912-13, Union Depot was built.

The new station was constructed in the Prairie Style popularized by Frank Lloyd Wright. The most distinctive feature of the building is its "mirror image" waiting rooms, designed to reflect the segregation laws adopted by Georgia and other states at the turn of the century.

Union Station served as the point of arrival and departure for three generations of Southwest Georgians. Soldiers departed for every American war from the Civil War through Vietnam from Union Station. It was at the station in 1961 that the painful process of integration began for Albany when the Freedom Riders arrived. In 1971, the last passenger train pulled out of Albany's Union Depot, leaving behind a silent, already run-down station.

Rather than let the old depot suffer the same fate as so many other Albany landmarks, like being razed or allowed to fall into decay, a group of citizens formed a historical preservation society dedicated to preserving what it could of old Albany.

In 1974, Thronateeska Heritage Foundation Inc. was formed with the merger of the Southwest Georgia Historical Society and the Albany Area Museum. Almost immediately its members began an effort to create a museum in the old passenger terminal.

For years, however, the old depot was used to house a hodgepodge of temporary exhibits and artifacts. Then in 1994, the dream of a functional museum came closer to reality when the citizens of Dougherty County passed a special-purpose local-option sales tax providing $750,000 for renovations to the train station.

The renovations were started in the fall of '97 and were completed in the spring of '98. This coincided with the installation of a professionally prepared exhibit.

"The theme of the exhibit is 'Community: A Journey of Discovery,'" Dr. Joseph H. Kitchens, executive director of Thronateeska Heritage Center says. "It tells not just the history of Albany, but it interprets Southwest Georgia as a community."

The 4,000-square-foot exhibit has a number of interactives for children and chronicles subjects like Indians, celebrations, and social life, transportation, education, and farming. Local architects Yielding, Wakeford & McGee did the design work for the new museum, while McDonald Contracting Inc. did the construction work, and Touch Design Inc. was responsible for the exhibit design and construction.

After the renovations, Thronateeska's board of directors decided to change the name of Union Station to the Discovery Depot, a name chosen to add excitement for visiting children.

With a mission statement "to preserve and examine our past, which both unites and divides us, in order to better understand the present and prepare effectively for the future," the Discovery Depot serves as the anchor for Thronateeska's Heritage Plaza, which also includes the Wetherbee Planetarium and the Science Discovery Center.

The purpose of the planetarium is to educate both

school children and adults about our solar system, while the Science Discovery Center showcases a number of interactive exhibits for children, including lessons on magnetism, gravity, and electricity.

The science center is housed in the old Railway Express Agency building. REA was the forerunner of today's air express services. It fueled the rise of the modern department store, as well as mail order houses like Sears and Roebuck. Another significant structure at Heritage Plaza is the old Tift Grocery Warehouse, which was originally the 1857 rail station.

Plans call for the old warehouse to be renovated and used as a transportation museum. Thronateeska owns a 1911 steam locomotive, two cabooses, and two other railroad cars. In addition, there is a model train exhibit—the only one in Georgia housed in a train car.

Looking to the future, Thronateeska is making the old rail station a center of community activity. The center's rental facilities have all been remodeled and are available for formal receptions and meetings. And, for less formal occasions, there are facilities for dances, parties, and meetings. ❧

Braided in the course of time, currents fold to weave a river. Generations surging past, live their stories . . . and together tell its course.

Cardiovascular Program in Southwest Georgia

p until January, 1983, patients in Albany had to travel to Atlanta, Tallahassee, or Jacksonville, Florida, for specialized cardiac care. Establishing a heart program in Southwest Georgia was no easy task, Dr. Freeman, a cardiothoracic surgeon, recalls. First, he had to garner local support for the idea, and then, he and the others had to get a state law changed that restricted offering cardiac services if such were offered within a three- or four-hour drive.

After a vigorous four-year campaign for a cardiac catheterization/open heart surgery program, the Georgia State Health Planning Agency approved Phoebe Putney's application. Doctors Michael Roberts and William Safley joined Dr. Freeman to lead the open heart surgical team while Dr. Jeffrey Hoopes was recruited from Atlanta to establish the cardiac catheterization lab. Through their efforts and those of many specialists who followed, Albany now has a full service, state-of-the-art cardiovascular program.

Dr. Jeffrey Hoopes performs a cardiac catheterization.

a tragic, unexpected death. Dr. Anthony Hoots and Dr. Charles Wayne Holley, the remaining partners of Cardiovascular Surgical Associates, have picked up the heavy load of cardiac, thoracic, and peripheral vascular surgery.

CARDIOLOGY ASSOCIATES, P.C.

Cardiology Associates, P.C. was established in 1982 by Dr. Jeffrey Hoopes who also opened the Cardiac Catheterization Lab at Phoebe Putney Memorial Hospital in January 1983. Since its inception, the practice has grown to five physician members, each of whom specializes in key areas.

Cardiac catheterizations are performed by four of the five physician members and numbered over 2,700 procedures in 1997. Dr. Craig Mitchell and Dr. Thomas Joiner specialize in coronary interventions. In 1997, over 600 coronary angioplasties were performed. 70 percent of which were combined with the placement of a coronary stent operation. Atherectomy, a procedure to "roto-rooter®" plaque from the arteries, may also be used. All coronary interventions, such as angioplasty, stenting, and atherectomy are performed in the cardiac catheterization laboratory.

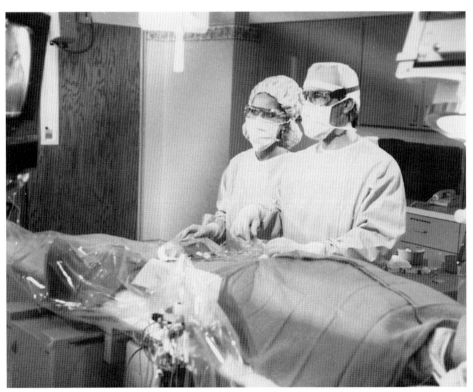

The physicians at Cardiology Associates, P.C. can place temporary pacemakers and Dr. Stephen Souther implants permanent pacemakers. Patients are then enrolled in a Pacemaker Clinic at Cardiology Associates for telephonic and office monitoring. Dr. Stephen Mitchell and Dr. Stephen Souther are nuclear cardiologists and each is certified to interpret Cardiolite, thallium, and MUGA studies. Dr. Stephen Mitchell and Dr. Souther perform transesophageal echocardiograms. This procedure is done when a transthoracic echocardiogram is insufficient or during valvular heart surgery.

CARDIOVASCULAR SURGICAL ASSOCIATES, P.C.

Dr. Roberts performed the first open heart surgery at Phoebe Putney Hospital in 1983 and was one of the founding surgeons of Albany's open heart surgical team. The surgical program has grown to include additional procedures and case volume.

1997 was a year of transition for Cardiovascular Surgical Associates, P.C. Founding member Dr. James Freeman retired and Dr. Michael Roberts had

HEART OF THE SOUTH CARDIAC INSTITUTE

Phoebe Putney Memorial Hospital combined with the physicians to form the Heart of the South Cardiac Institute. In the early 1980s, the hospital was approved for a heart catheterization lab and an open heart program. Not long afterwards, Phoebe was also selected as a site for training cardiology and pulmonary technologists. It was also the first hospital in the region to upgrade to Doppler and color-flow echocardiography, a system to allow doctors to observe blood flow through the heart.

Along with the continuous inclusion of new techniques and better technology internally, Phoebe was growing regionally as well. In February 1989, Phoebe launched the Heart of the South Cardiac Network, a cooperative effort by Phoebe and nine area hospitals. Phoebe serves as the anchor of this regional emergency network, the first of its kind in Georgia. A mobile intensive care unit was custom-built at a cost of $160,000 to transport patients from outlying hospitals to Phoebe for tertiary care. The mobile unit has the same equipment and staff as the CCU, which is not available in a standard emergency transport.

To improve the identification and treatment of heart disease, Phoebe Putney opened the Chest Pain Center at the hospital in 1998. The center is dedicated solely to caring for heart patients on an emergency basis.

Together, Cardiovascular Surgical Associates, P.C., Cardiology Associates, P.C., and Phoebe Putney Memorial Hospital collectively created medical and surgical services that are among the finest in the

Southeastern United States. The collaborative effort has brought high-tech medicine to Southwest Georgia and eliminated the need for patients to leave their community for medical services. All members of the cardiovascular team have pride in their program in delivering the right care, at the right place, and at the right time. ❧

Dr. Craig Mitchell and Dr. Thomas Joiner in Cath Lab.

Mobile Coronary Care Unit.

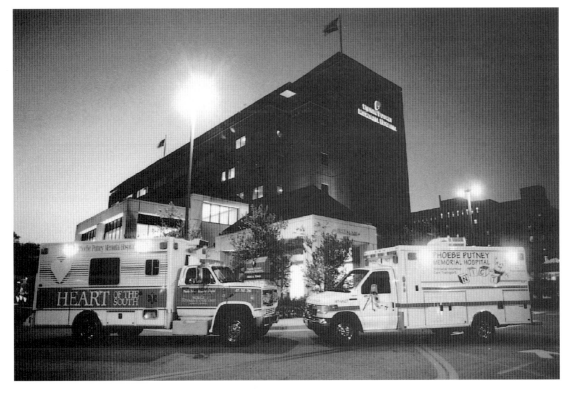

Palmyra Medical Centers

On February 1, 1971, Palmyra Park Hospital opened its doors, becoming known as Palmyra Medical Centers in 1986.

*I*n the late '60s health care in southwest Georgia was at a point of near crisis. Albany, the regional hub of southwest Georgia, had only one hospital serving the area, and it became more evident with each passing day that a second hospital was needed to handle the growing demand for quality service.

"The only hospital in town was overcrowded back then," recalls Dr. Tom Johnson, now retired. "Patients were in the halls waiting for rooms to become available. Then one day this guy calls me and says he wanted to build another hospital in Albany. I said, 'What's the catch?'"

That "guy" was Dr. Thomas Frist Jr. of Hospital Corporation of America (HCA), and the only "catch" was a commitment to superior health care—a commitment Dr. Johnson and others were eager to support.

Pastureland located on a road named for an old settlement called Palmyra was eventually picked as the building site. It took two years to build and $7 million of private investor capital to complete the project.

On February 1, 1971, Palmyra Park Hospital opened its doors. In 1986, the hospital became known

as Palmyra Medical Centers, as it's known today, to reflect the growing number of services offered.

Both Albany hospitals boast the latest technology and procedures, enhancing every service they offer. Competition also encouraged the hospitals to seek out areas of specialty, like the Palmyra Regional Rehabilitation Center and the NOR Institute.

Palmyra Rehabilitation Center, opened in 1987, is the only comprehensive Level 3 program within the 125-mile radius of southwest Georgia and southeast Alabama, where patients get an intense three hours of therapy daily. It provides both outpatient and inpatient physical rehabilitation in an acute care hospital setting.

Patients are encouraged to be as independent as they can be. Palmyra helps patients achieve this goal through its "outcomes-based" program. First, an ultimate goal is determined, which is generally independence. Then, shorter, progressive goals are established for each patient, with the focus aimed at reaching one goal at a time.

The Palmyra Sports Medicine Center opened in June 1991 and a Diabetes Treatment Center followed in 1992.

In 1994, Palmyra introduced the NOR Institute, an innovative, multidisciplinary facility that integrates neuroscience, orthopedics, and rehabilitation for a logical progression from preadmission to post-discharge. Also that year, outpatient services expanded with the opening of the new Outpatient Surgical Center. These specialized treatment centers boost the overall quality of health care in a region that probably would not have evolved to this point with just one hospital in town, according to Palmyra Chief Executive Officer Allen Golson.

"Albany always will be a two-hospital town," Golson says. "All we are going to do is make each other better. We are both just as much a part of the community as the other."

When Palmyra Park opened, the hospital offered complete medical and surgical services, with six large operating rooms, four X-ray rooms, a Nuclear Medicine department, an eight-bed Coronary Unit, a 10-bed Intensive Care Unit, and complete food preparation and service facilities. The 223 beds included 123 private rooms and a landscaped roof garden provided ambulatory and wheelchair patients an exercise and recreational area in "the fresh air and sunshine." Today the hospital boasts 248 beds.

By Palmyra's fifth anniversary in 1976, 40,000 patients had been treated. To accommodate the increasing demand for services, the hospital launched a series of expansions that show no signs of letting up.

An emergency department was added in 1978. A little more than a decade later, that same department

When Palmyra opened, its 223 beds included 123 private rooms and a landscaped roof garden provided ambulatory and wheelchair patients an exercise and recreational area, Today the hospital boasts 248 beds.

evolved into a major Emergency Center. A $9.9-million hospital expansion in 1983 added Outpatient Surgery and a Cardiac Rehabilitation Program.

When Palmyra Park evolved into Palmyra Medical Centers in 1986, the goal was to better represent the numerous "medical centers" throughout the organization, such as the Emergency Center, the Ambulatory Surgery Center, the Diagnostic Imaging Center, the Stone Treatment Center, the Sleep Studies Center, the Laser Center, the Pain Treatment Center, the Palmyra Regional Rehabilitation Center, the Center for Occupational Health, the NOR Institute, and the GoodLife Sports Medicine Center.

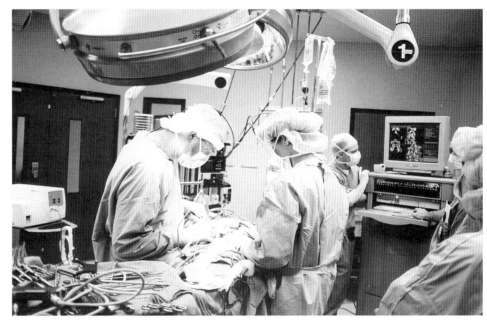

One "center" the hospital doesn't have yet, but is counting on for the future, is a maternity ward. According to Golson, providing obstetrical services is a main goal for the hospital.

"We are very positive about obstetrics in our future," he says. "In fact, I'm so positive that we've had a building and floor plan developed."

Bringing a maternity center to Palmyra hasn't been an easy proposition. The state of Georgia has a law that requires hospitals and other medical institutions to provide proof the services they want to offer in an area are needed.

While the OB challenge continues, Palmyra doesn't rest. Throughout its history, the hospital has been a staunch supporter of numerous community causes and organizations. In 1997 alone, Palmyra paid more than $8 million in taxes, charity, and uncompensated care. The hospital contributes more than $90,000 to local charitable organizations annually. Palmyra associates are also active in various civic groups in the communities in which they live.

Additionally, Palmyra implements a broad spectrum of strategies from educational programs to wellness programs to improve the overall health of the community.

From the beginning, Palmyra's goal has been to provide first-rate health care to the people of southwest Georgia. Since that time, the administration and associates never have lost sight of that goal.

Reflecting on the hospital's past success, Golson says the best is yet to come.

"We plan to be here 100 years from now, still putting quality first, cost second and to continue playing the role of the good corporate citizen," he says. ❧

From the beginning, Palmyra's goal has been to provide first-rate health care to the people of southwest Georgia. Today that includes state-of-the-art operating rooms and equipment.

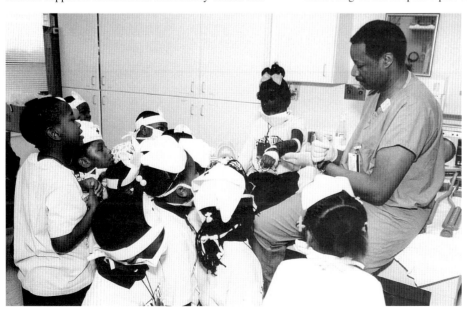

Palmyra implements a broad spectrum of strategies from educational programs to wellness programs to improve the overall health of the community.

Brooks Communications

*Brooks
Communications
is now home to
WKAK, WALG,
WEGC, and WJAD
radio stations only
since* Albany
Magazine's *spin-off
in January 1998.*

What began as merely an investment for one Albany man five years ago, has turned into southwest Georgia's dominant communications group.

In 1961, Bob Brooks enlisted in the Army, which brought him to the Albany area. Stationed in Sylvester, Brooks met his future wife, Josephine LaVerne Butler, at an Albany drive-in restaurant in 1963. Four months later, the couple were married. After his marriage, Brooks was transferred to Turner Field in Albany.

After being discharged in 1964, Brooks went to work for his father-in-law, Joe Butler, delivering furniture and appliances. Three years later, Brooks quit Butler Johnson Furniture and went to work for Miles Furniture. Brooks was eventually promoted to general manager at Miles, but after 13 years with the company, he ventured out on his own, opening Brooks Furniture and Brookline, an upholstery manufacturing company.

While still working for Miles, Brooks began investing in residential and commercial properties, as well as investing in some other business ventures.

Having already made a name for himself in the real estate and furniture businesses, in November 1993, Brooks decided to try his hand in the broadcasting business.

Platinum Broadcasting had been trying to sell two Albany radio stations—WKAK, 101.7, and WALG, 1590 AM—for several years, with no luck.

Brooks bought the struggling stations, which were located on Dunbar Lane. The stations turned out to be such a good investment for Brooks, in April 1997, he purchased two more, WJAD, 103.5, and WEGC, 107.7. The stations were located in Albany Towers.

Six months later, all four stations were moved into the old First State Bank building at the corner of Broad Avenue and Slappey Boulevard. Each of the stations represents a different musical format, from country and rock, to oldies and talk. All four stations operate under the umbrella company Brooks Communications, according to general manager Dean Burke.

"Collectively, our stations reach 67 percent of the total listening audience in Dougherty and Lee Counties," Burke says. "All of our shows are ranked #1 in their format."

Competition in the radio business in the Albany market is fierce, according to Burke, with each format competing with at least two similar stations. The country station competes against three other stations.

Burke credits his salespeople, on-air talent, and staff with the stations' success. At any quarter hour, there are more than 100,000 people listening to a Brooks Communications station, he says.

The stations have grown from 9 employees to 28, and Burke said he's in the process of doubling his sales staff to 10.

"We're having the best year we've ever had," he says.

And Burke said he knows the stations have the community to thank for their success. Because of that, all four stations are actively involved with several local charities.

"We do more work for the community and charities than our competitors put together," he says. "No other station is more involved in the community than we are."

Burke estimates the stations provide more than half-a-million dollars to local charities in donations and free air time. The American Cancer Society and Easter Seals have recognized Brooks Communications as the recipient of their Media Award for supplying the most free air time to the charities.

"I think if you live in the community, you've got to be involved in the community," he says. "I think that's a big part of why we're #1; we're always seen."

While the radio stations may be the most visible part of Brooks Communications, they are not the only component.

In March 1995, company executives were discussing marketing tools for the country music station. The discussion started with talk of a glossy newsletter, but as the brainstorming session continued, it soon became apparent what they were talking about was much more than a newsletter.

"The topics we were coming up with were for a magazine," Michael Brooks, editor-in-chief/creative director of *Albany Magazine* says. "We were limiting ourselves to country radio demographics. I didn't want to do just a country radio newsletter. We can still market the radio stations through the magazine, but this way there's the potential to bring in new listeners."

And so *Albany Magazine* was born.

The magazine was originally part of the umbrella group, Brooks Communications, but in January of 1998, the magazine was spun-off into Brooks Advertising and Design Co., or BAD Co. The bi-monthly publication prints 10,000 copies of each edition, with subscriptions for more than 5,000 of those copies.

"I want readers to know Albany can be one of the most interesting places to live," Brooks says. "I want *Albany Magazine* to be representative of Albany and what it has to offer, without a bunch of fluff."

Albany Magazine celebrated its third anniversary in 1998, and despite its youth, in its first professional showing last year, the magazine garnered two golds and one silver award from the Georgia Magazine Association and this year, the city's magazine swept the awards with four golds and one silver.

As the Albany area continues to grow and prosper, the Brooks Communications group looks forward to continuing to serve the community and mirroring its success. ❧

Award-winning photography, design, and editorial account for Albany Magazine*'s success at the 1998 GAMMA Awards.*

Albany Electric

Three weeks after Ronnie Hinson started Albany Electric, the company was awarded a large industrial project. Good news for any upstart venture, but there were a few obstacles in his way.

"We bid on and were awarded this large industrial project before we had any employees, and our banking, bonding, insurance, and suppliers were not in place," Hinson recalls with a chuckle. "The job had to be completed in 90 days, and we did that."

That was back in 1983.

Since then, Albany Electric has grown from a 23-employee company with an annual payroll of $425,000 to today's 192 employees and a payroll approaching $6 million.

While the electrical contracting business is a cut-throat industry, Hinson says he is proud of his company's roots.

"The company I was working for at the time was discontinuing operations after the president died," he says. "We started the company in a very ethical and professional way. Most of these type businesses started by stealing the customers of the other company, but we didn't do that."

What Hinson, Bill Thompson, Jerry Williams, and Jerome Harrison did do was carve a niche for themselves and Albany Electric in a business that was dominated by established companies.

"We will do anything from a small residential service call to a multimillion-dollar project," Hinson says, "and we do each one regardless of the size dedicated to customer satisfaction."

Albany Electric has done some of the biggest jobs in Albany, as well as some of the most important, including restoration work at Albany State University following the disastrous Flood of '94, work on the Municipal Auditorium, and the electrical work for the surgery expansion at Phoebe Putney Memorial Hospital.

"The thing that we do differently now than we have done in the past is, we do a lot of telecommunications work—computer and telecommunications wiring and cabling," Hinson says. "Wiring a building now for data is almost getting to the level of wiring a building for power and lights."

While the company is only in the first generation of ownership, Albany Electric has already created a legacy of giving to charitable organizations in Dougherty County.

At the same time Hinson formed the company in 1983, he also established a charitable foundation.

"We created the foundation so if we made some money, we could support the community," he says. "It's just a way to give back something to the community."

The foundation supports local schools and youth sports, but in addition to that monetary help, Albany Electric works with the school system to prepare students for jobs in electrical contracting.

Albany Electric sponsors a youth apprenticeship program, where students can work for the company part-time while they're still in school, and once they graduate, they can go straight to work with the company's apprenticeship program.

To date, there are 19 students in southwest Georgia participating in the school-to-work program at Albany Electric, while 46 people are employed full-time with the company's apprenticeship program.

"We've got a 25-year plan on how big the company will be and how many employees we'll need," Hinson says. "We love this area and our whole company is built strictly by the people from here, and we're a people business." ❧

Since 1983 Albany Electric has grown from a 23-employee company with an annual payroll of $425,000 to today's 192 employees and a payroll approaching $6 million.

Merts, Inc.

*I*n the 1950s, Milton Merts was employed as treasurer and construction equipment salesman for Merts Equipment Co.

He and Sales Manager Bill Coppedge saw that concrete producers in the Southeast needed equipment and services not currently available to them. The producers needed a specialized steel fabricator, and they also needed someone to erect the equipment and help them put it in service with minimum delay and trouble.

Merts and Coppedge responded to those needs.

Merts produced the first decumulative aggregate batching system, which became the granddaddy of all modern low profile concrete batching plants. Merts also developed the batcher charging unit, which combines aggregate storage bins and their associated conveyors into one portable unit. Merts and Coppedge also participated in the early beginnings of automatic batching of materials. They provided load cells for weighing back when load cells were handmade one at a time and control relays were the size of softballs.

They assembled a talented crew of fabricators and erectors and started operations as a division of Merts Equipment Co.

Roy Brown was their first Production Manager. Brown had a talent for turning customers' dreams into steel.

Merts and Coppedge's first welding and fabrication shop was located in one end of an airplane hanger at the local airport. The production facility and office later moved to the old Darr Homes location across Newton Road from the airport.

The single theme of providing new, better, and specialized services for their concrete-producing customers has been the guiding theme of Merts ever since.

In 1970, the Merts Equipment Co. fabrication division spun off from its parent company and became known as Merts Manufacturing and Engineering Co. The name was later shortened to Merts, Inc.

Eleven years later in 1981, the company moved from the old Darr Homes location to its present site at 1939 Ledo Road.

Milton Merts now serves as Chairman of the Board, while Joel Johnson, a 20-year employee of the company, serves as President and CEO. Anne Williamson, who joined the company as office manager in 1963, is now Merts Vice President. Bill Mangum joined the company in 1987 as sales manager. Bill has had forty-six years experience in the building materials and concrete industries.

Throughout its history, Merts has continued to develop a highly skilled organization capable of solving specialized problems of concrete producers.

The conveying, batching, dispatching, and inventory control of material is now mostly computer controlled. Standard load cells have replaced mechanical scales.

Merts ships equipment into many parts of the country east of the Mississippi, the Caribbean Islands, and Mexico. ❧

Then ...

... and now.

ALLTEL Communications

Groundbreaking for new state-of-the-art facility in Albany. ALLTEL in 1998—200 employees and over 90,000 customers.

Ten years ago, the cellular phone industry in southwest Georgia was nonexistent. Today, everyone from business professionals to soccer moms accessorize with a cellular phone, contributing to the fastest growing industry in the history of the United States.

ALLTEL Corp., the largest provider of cellular service in Albany and southwest Georgia, is a customer-focused, information technology company which has provided state-of-the-art wireline and wireless communications and information services to its customers for 25 years.

In 1983, the Federal Communications Commission issued the first cellular operating licenses. ALLTEL, which had previously operated land line telephone services in Albany, was awarded the operating licenses for the Albany metropolitan area and several surrounding regional areas.

Operations in Albany began in May, 1988, with a meeting of civic and business leaders at the Albany Museum of Art. ALLTEL's humble beginning in Albany included only five employees, with a monthly payroll of less than $10,000.

Today, ALLTEL's cellular network consists of more than 65 towers, 10 of which were built in 1997 alone, covering a 43-county area.

"The phone has evolved from a 12-pound brick to something you can wear on your belt," ALLTEL Vice President and General Manager Paul Bowersock says.

In the beginning, a good sales week for the company was four to five activations a week. In 1997, monthly new activations in southwest Georgia regularly exceeded 2,000 units. ALLTEL sold over 91 million minutes of airtime in 1997, and wireless usage continues to increase.

"ALLTEL'S Albany area customer base has grown from zero to more than 90,000 in just 10 years," Bowersock says, "exceeding our wildest expectations."

To provide easy sales access, quality network reliability, and superior customer service, ALLTEL now employs nearly 200 personnel all around south Georgia with an annual payroll exceeding $6 million.

While ALLTEL prides itself on the outstanding quality of the products and services it provides to its customers, the company also firmly believes in outstanding corporate citizenship.

During its 10 years in Albany, ALLTEL has been a major sponsor of the Chehaw Indian Festival, River Days Festival, the American Heart Association, the American Cancer Society, the Nancy Lopez Hospice Golf Tournament, the March of Dimes, and the Chamber of Commerce. During the devastating flood of 1994, as well as the flood of 1998, ALLTEL provided hundreds of cellular phones to emergency assistance agencies at all levels, as well as free airtime. Additionally, ALLTEL employees were personally involved in all aspects of the recovery effort.

"ALLTEL Corporation and our employees are proud to be part of the Albany and Flint River area business heritage," Bowersock says. "In the future we look forward to bringing our customers in Albany the latest in technological advances in wireline and wireless communications and information services while continuing to strengthen our already strong commitment to the communities we serve." ❧

ALLTEL in 1988— one vehicle, five employees, and less than one hundred customers.

Albany Museum of Art

*I*n less than 40 years, the Albany Museum of Art has become a beacon of culture and education in southwest Georgia.

Founded in the 1960s as the Southwest Georgia Art Association, the foundation of today's museum was housed in a defunct hosiery mill on Oglethorpe Boulevard. Less than 10 years later, through the generosity of W. Banks Haley Jr., a gallery was opened on municipally donated land.

The Banks Halley Gallery opened with an all-volunteer staff and hosted a variety of exhibitions.

The Banks Halley Gallery continued to grow and in 1980, a fundraising campaign was initiated that raised $1.2 million for the construction of the current facility, which opened in 1984 with an exhibition from the Phillips Gallery of Art in Washington, D.C. The AMA continues to present a wide variety of changing exhibitions, including French and American Impressionism, Breaking Barries: Recent American Craft, and I Dream a World, Black Women who Changed America.

For a relatively new regional museum, the Albany Museum of Art has already assembled impressive collections.

The museum has one of the largest collections of sub-Saharan African art in the Southeast. Holdings include a wealth of masks, along with sculpture, pottery, baskets, textiles, jewelry, and gold weights.

Albany resident Stella Davis donated several hundred objects of African art to the museum in the 1980s, while her cousin, Michael Davis, donated more than 150 16th and 17th century drawings.

"Our mission is to collect 19th and 20th century African, American, and European art," says Tim Close, the current Executive Director. "We have probably one of the best African collections in the Southeast."

According to Close, Mrs. Davis was a foreign service officer in Africa at one time, while her cousin Michael traveled throughout Europe and collected drawings.

"They amassed collections independently of each other and wanted to see them preserved," Close says of the Davises' motives for donating the collections. "Art was also a way to give back to their community."

Other major contributors to the museum's permanent collection were Dr. and Mrs. Henry Goodyear, who donated important paintings by American artists Joseph Henry Sharp and Edward Potthast to start AMA's collection. Later in 1998, Mr. and Mrs. Raymond F. Evans, former owners of a private hunting preserve in Albany, generously contributed works by sporting artists including Aiden Lassell Ripley and enabled the museum to open the Raymond F. Evans Sporting Art Gallery.

The American and European collections include paintings by Lawson, Potthast, and Sharp. Contemporary art is represented with works by Hans Hoffman, Moses Soyer, Andy Warhol, Robert Rauschenberg, Dale Chihuly, and Philip Evergood. The museum also houses a growing photography collection that is comprised of portraits of modern artists.

"It's a major coup for a city the size of Albany to have a museum of this quality and stature," Close says. "We're also blessed to have the support of the citizens of Albany to make this happen."

Today, the Albany Museum of Art is the only institution accredited by the American Association of Museums within a 100-mile radius. Annually, more than 30,000 adults and children visit the museum to take part in its many educational programs.

"As a regional art museum, we have a real responsibility to educate people about the arts and how the arts are important in our lives," Close says. ❧

The Albany Museum of Art is the only institution accredited by the American Association of Museums within a 100-mile radius.

Miller Brewing Co.

*A*once abandoned airfield is today home to one of Dougherty County's—and the state's—industrial powerhouses.

Turning abandoned pieces of property into thriving enterprises is a part of the history of Miller Brewing Co.

Founded in 1855 by Frederick Miller, Miller Brewing Co. traces its roots to Milwaukee, where the German immigrant paid $8,000 for the Plank Road Brewery—a five-year-old brewery abandoned in 1854.

The Plank Road Brewery—now the Milwaukee Brewery—was located several miles west of Milwaukee in the Menomonee Valley. This location proved ideal for its nearness to a good water source and to raw materials grown on surrounding farms.

Similarly, it was an abundant supply of water, among other things, that brought Miller to Albany in 1979.

In addition to an ample water supply, the company was also looking for a central location to serve the Southeast and adequate transportation. Albany had all three.

The combination of criteria was found on a more than 1700-acre tract of land known as Turner Air Field.

The Navy abandoned the air field in the mid-70s, creating a huge economic and social black hole. Less than six years later, however, Miller came to town and constructed a 28-acre plant that today is among the largest employers in the Albany area.

Employing 630 people, Miller is an integral part of Albany and the state of Georgia. Locally, the plant produces $28 million in wages and benefits for Albany's

Miller Brewing Company is an integral part of Albany and the state of Georgia. With 630 employees and a payroll of more than $28 million, Miller Brewing is among the largest employers in the Albany area.

economy. The statewide economic impact totals more than $200 million, and in 1997, the plant paid more than $104 million in federal excise taxes. That's in addition to another $30 million the company pays in local and state taxes and fees.

Each year Miller produces more than 6 million barrels of beer at its Albany brewery. The plant brews Miller's whole line of beer products, including Miller Lite, Miller High Life, Miller High Life Light, Miller Genuine Draft, Ice House, Red Dog, Magnum, MeisterBräu, and Milwaukee's Best.

Miller Brewing is committed to supporting the communities where it does business. To that end, the Albany plant has made generous financial contributions to a host of charitable groups, nonprofit organizations, scholarship funds, and community development projects in the state, including Habitat for Humanity, a statewide hunger initiative called "Fighting Hunger in Georgia," and "Tools for Success®," a Miller-sponsored program which addresses skilled labor shortages by helping put technical graduates to work, equipping them with the tools they need in their professions.

As the twenty-first century nears, Miller looks forward to continuing its mission statement of satisfying customer requirements by effectively developing and utilizing human and physical resources through cooperation and teamwork to safely and consistently produce the highest quality beverages at the lowest possible cost. ❧

Procter & Gamble Paper Products Co.

One of Procter & Gamble's paper machines.

*W*hat was once a pecan orchard, today is home to the largest producer of tissue and towel products in the world. The Albany Procter & Gamble Paper Products Co. plant began operation in Dougherty County in December of 1972 and has been going strong ever since.

More than a quarter of a century ago, Cincinnati, Ohio-based Procter & Gamble was looking for a site in the Southeast, and Dougherty County had good availability of ground water for making paper and was sufficiently close enough to the interstate to get their products out in an efficient manner.

"The first plant manager was John Feldman," Public Affairs Manager Guy Griswold says. "He was a visionary person, bringing diverse cultures together, which hadn't been done in southwest Georgia before."

By the end of 1973, employment at the plant had risen to 600, with an annual payroll of $5 million. Today the plant employs about 1,600 people and boasts a more than $70-million payroll. The Albany plant produces Bounty paper towels and Charmin

bathroom tissues. During its 26 year history, Pampers, Luvs, and Rely have also been produced at the site.

Today, Dougherty County still has a plentiful water supply, a large labor pool and adequate transportation, and all of that has helped make the Albany plant one of the most efficient in the Procter & Gamble family.

The company's confidence in the Albany plant can be seen in the millions of dollars spent on capital expansion and improvements at the facility. Since 1994, $400 million in capital expansion has been invested at the Albany plant, while another $100 million has been spent on equipment upgrades.

Ground was broken for the plant's sixth papermaking machine in 1996, on the heels of a fifth machine, which began operating in December of 1996. The two expansions created more than 250 jobs. Once #6 is operational, the Albany plant will add about 65,000 tons of annual capacity to its production of Charmin and Charmin Ultra toilet tissue and Bounty paper towels.

With the completion of #6 and the associated converting equipment, the Albany plant will be the largest volume tissue-towel producer in the world.

"We've been building new capacity as fast as we can, and we're still having difficulty keeping up with demand for our products," Griswold says.

That demand helped the Albany plant celebrate 25 years in Albany in 1997. And while no one knows what the future holds, passing that milestone bodes well for the future of P&G's Albany plant.

"We're consistently gaining market share with our products," he says. "We're producing products with superior quality and performance, so consumers are choosing our products over our competitor's. The company is constantly developing new products because we have to continue to grow, and some of those are bound to be produced here in Albany."

Procter & Gamble's Albany plant.

Security Bank and Trust Company

The current main office of Security Bank, located on Pine Avenue.

The founding directors of Security Bank include {seated left to right) John L. Moulton, Dr. John S. Inman, Jr., John M. Beauchamp, E. Clifton Lancaster, (standing left to right) S. Thomas Walden, Joe T. Brashears, Lewis S. Thompson, III, Dr. H. Gordon Davis, Jr., and Dr. J.H. Sharman, Sr.

*I*n the late 1960s a group of Albany area businessmen, through a series of meetings, began to formulate ideas and plans that would result in the formation of Security Bank and Trust Company. Dr. John S. Inman Jr. was named chairman of the organization committee. Each organizing director put up $30,000 in organizing expenses and initial capital for the bank. Once the charter was approved by the State of Georgia, each director was charged with selling shares of stock in the new bank to friends and business acquaintances. It proved to be an opportune time for organizing a bank, as the Albany area was growing in population and enjoying new industries coming into the area. There was also a very strong loan demand in the community at this time, ultimately proving that organizing the new bank was a good investment opportunity. Ultimately, the directors were successful in their efforts to sell the bank's stock, convincing several hundred investors to join with them. Today, for the lucky individuals who did purchase shares of the original stock of Security Bank, in 1997 a $2,000 original investment, excluding reinvestment of dividends, was worth approximately $600,000. In January 1970, Security Bank was incorporated at $20 a share and capitalized at $1,000,000. The bank has been profitable every month since it opened. The bank was able to start paying a dividend on the stock earlier into its beginning operation. Today, the bank has assets of more than $210,000,000 and trust assets of approximately $90,000,000.

The bank was chartered in April of 1970, and it opened in August at 700 Pine Avenue in a mobile

office. This temporary facility housed Albany's newest bank, while a main office was constructed at the corner of Pine Avenue and Davis Street.

Under the direction of John Inman, John L. Moulton, E. Clifton Lancaster, John Beauchamp, Tommy Walden, Joe T. Brashears, L. S. Thompson, Dr. H. Gordon Davis Jr., Dr. J. H. Sharman, and K. B. Hodges Jr., Security Bank opened its new headquarters in May of 1971.

John L. Moulton was elected chairman of the board, and E. Clifton Lancaster was named president of the bank. The bank grew quickly and prospered throughout the 1970s, bringing about the need for additional capital, which was raised in 1975 through a secondary stock offering. In 1979, Security Bank was acquired in a three-for-one stock exchange by CB&T Bancshares in Columbus, Georgia. Today CB&T Bancshares is known as Synovus Financial Corp.

The bank's partnership with Synovus has offered it vast opportunities to continue to grow and prosper. However, its leadership has never lost sight of the importance of community involvement.

From its inception, the bank has been actively involved in community affairs, with officers and staff serving in leadership roles with virtually every community, civic, cultural, and charitable organization in Albany. In April of 1992, the bank moved its main office to 401 Pine Avenue and simultaneously donated a historic house adjacent to its new headquarters to Thronateeska Heritage Center, paying for the moving of the building to the center. Today, the house serves as an educational and technical center benefiting school children from across southwest Georgia.

"It is the tradition of excellence that is the cornerstone of Security Bank and Trust's commitment to serve this community as other Synovus affiliates serve the communities in which they are located," Security Bank President Mark Davis states. ❧

Buffalo Rock Company

*I*n the backyard of the world headquarters of Coca-Cola, Buffalo Rock Pepsi has grown to be the soft drink of choice in southwest Georgia.

"Coca-Cola was dominant in the area when Buffalo Rock bought out the franchise in 1985," says Administrative Office Manager Sharon Hembree, "but they are no longer dominant now."

A 20-year employee, Ms. Hembree says when Birmingham, Alabama-based Buffalo Rock bought Albany's Pepsi franchise, the company employed 35 people and serviced only seven routes. Today, the company boasts 116 employees and services 15 routes in 13 southwest Georgia counties. Sales for 1997 totaled $16 million.

A three- or four-man team works in any given territory, and under this system, someone is in every store Buffalo Rock services on a daily basis.

"Customer service is one of the things Buffalo Rock prides itself on," Ms. Hembree said. "We are a 24-hour-a-day company on call for product and service."

And Buffalo Rock has not only won over the taste buds of southwest Georgians, but it's won their hearts as well. The walls of the main office building on Randolph Street are lined with plaques of appreciation from various civic and charitable organizations from across the region, including the March of Dimes and Easter Seals.

"We support many nonprofit organizations," Cindy Senn says. "We are very much a part of the communities we serve."

Throughout its 13-year history in southwest Georgia, Buffalo Rock has continually expanded not only its product line, but its physical plant as well.

Back in 1985, the Randolph Street location housed one office building and one warehouse. Today there are three warehouses on the property, and Buffalo Rock offers an expanded product line that includes 7-Up, Sunkist, Dr. Pepper, coffee, tea, Pepsi-freeze, Canada Dry ginger ale, and Sunny Delight.

"This division was the number one per capita consumption distributor in the nation for Sunny Delight sales in 1997," Ms. Hembree says. "We were number one for per capita consumption within the Buffalo Rock franchise."

New products and services have long been a part of the continued expansion and growth of Buffalo Rock, and in 1990, Buffalo Rock Albany branched into full-line vending service.

Everything Buffalo Rock sells as part of its full-line vending service is made in a kitchen on-site, from barbecue and hot dogs to sandwiches and snacks. The on-site kitchen was added in 1996.

"We used to have to get our food for the vending machines from Dothan, Alabama, but now we prepare everything fresh, on-site daily," Ms. Hembree says.

With the on-site kitchen, Buffalo Rock then branched into the catering business.

"We've catered Marine balls, chamber breakfasts, and Cooper Tire Company's annual picnic," Ms. Hembree says.

In addition, the company also operates four off-site cafeterias at some of southwest Georgia's largest industries.

Buffalo Rock Company has been in operation for almost 100 years, spanning five generations of the Lee Family. Today, James C. Lee, Jr. is Chairman, his son, James C. Lee, III, is President and Chief Executive Officer, and Jamie Lee, his granddaughter, is Coordinator of Corporate Affairs. ❧

Yielding, Wakeford & McGee Architects

Radium Springs Casino.

Community Services-Theater Building, Darton College.

Beginning in the heart of downtown Albany and walking in any direction through the city and county, you will encounter buildings, old and new, which reflect the creative touch of the design team of Yielding, Wakeford and McGee Architects. Since 1975, this firm has provided effective leadership in architectural and interior design on projects ranging from private residences to historic renovation/restoration to multi-story institutional buildings. In doing so, the architects of YWM have left their mark on the history and growth of Southwest Georgia.

They started small in 1975, scrubbing, painting, and adapting space in an old building downtown for their first office. They had worked together for several years for a local architectural firm and had hoped one day to have their own businesses. When their employer encountered financial problems, his young associates decided that they would be better off on their own. In spite of the economic recession which had a grip on

the building industry that year, J.M. Yielding and Mack Wakeford borrowed the money to get started, hung out their sign, and prepared for their first commission.

While they were still in the midst of office set-up, a local developer saw the sign and came in to ask if they were open. He gave them a small remodeling design job for some rental property he had purchased—and they have not paused in their work since. The design of a tennis clubhouse followed quickly, and in the next year, they got the big break they had hoped for. The firm was hired to design the transformation of the historic Gordon Hotel into a modern, efficient municipal headquarters for the Water, Gas, and Light Commission. Their success in redesigning the structure to yield maximum business efficiency while preserving the unique decorative elements of the well-known building established the firm in the Albany market.

Twenty-three years later, Yielding, Wakeford, and long-time associate, now partner, Derrell McGee have expanded their staff and scope of operations, but they continue to set the tone for sensitive, innovative building design in Albany. The firm is responsible for the adaptive reuse of the AGE Federal Credit Union's administrative offices, the WG&L Annex, the Dougherty County Central Library, the Union Depot at Thronateeska Heritage Center, the reconstruction of the historic Radium Springs Casino, and their own investment in urban renewal, the YWM offices on Heritage Plaza. They have won awards for their design of Veterans Park on the riverfront and the City of Albany's Business and Technology Center nearby. Certainly not limited to the downtown center, their designs also include Albany Technical Institute's Industrial Technology Center, the Child Care Center of Phoebe Putney Memorial Hospital, Albany Orthopedic Center for Palmyra Medical Centers, the Allied Health/Community Services building at Darton College, and Peace Hall and the new Student Mall at Albany State University. Additional design awards for the Albany Beverage Company and the Albany Museum of Art acknowledge the firm's flair for blending traditional and contemporary design elements to meet the needs of their clients and to reflect the character of Albany—both historic and progressive, modest and grand, respectful of the past and enthusiastic for the future. ❧

Albany Regional Plastic Surgery

lbany's preeminent medical establishment attracted Dr. Stanley J. Moye, owner and operator of Albany Regional Plastic Surgery. Dr. Moye's comprehensive approach to plastic surgery is reflected in his dual certification by both the American Board of Plastic Surgery and the American Board of Surgery. He is also a fellow of the American College of Surgeons and an active member of the American Society of Plastic and Reconstructive Surgeons.

Stanley J. Moye, M.D., owner and operator of Albany Regional Plastic Surgery.

Dr. Moye grew up on a south Georgia farm. After receiving his undergraduate and medical degrees from Emory University and completing nine years of postgraduate medical training, he established his practice in Albany. Because of the regional superiority of its medical community he chose Albany for the home of his progressive, new plastic surgery practice in 1992. Since that time, he has pioneered the practice of breast reconstruction surgery immediately following mastectomy, as well as laser facial resurfacing. His practice focuses on cosmetic surgery and on surgery to restore the breast after mastectomy.

In 1997 Dr. Moye instituted his in-office surgical facility, which allows for the most confidential, convenient, and personalized setting possible. Procedures offered in his office include laser facial resurfacing, liposuction, tummy-tuck, breast enlargement or lift, face lift, neck lift, and eyelid lift. It is equipped to offer endoscopic brow or forehead lifts. Patients even have the option of spending the night after surgery in a recovery suite with the assistance of a knowledgeable staff for their care.

Albany Regional Plastic Surgery is southwest Georgia's only center offering Endermologie. This nonsurgical, therapeutic massage tones the skin and improves the appearance of cellulite. This treatment also dramatically speeds a patient's recovery from surgery. Dr. Moye is pleased to be one of the few surgeons incorporating Endermologie into a patient's postoperative care.

Continually striving to offer patients the latest technologies and procedures available, Dr. Moye is bringing to Albany the facilities and convenience found in larger metropolitan areas. ❧

Bibliography

Anonymous. *History and Reminiscences of Dougherty County*. Compiled by the Thronateeska Chapter of the Daughters of the American Revolution. Albany, Georgia. 1924.

Anonymous. Inventory of the County Archives of Georgia. Georgia Historical Records Survey, Works Progress Administration. Atlanta: Georgia Historical Records Survey, 1941.

Anonymous. *Journal of Southwest Georgia History*. Albany, Georgia: published annually by Albany State University and Thronateeska Heritage Center since 1983.

Bacon, Mary Ellen. *Albany on the Flint: Indians to Industry. 1836-1946*. Albany, Georgia: Town Committee of the Colonial Dames of America in the State of Georgia, 1970.

Clive, Carolyn, et al. *Glancing Backward*. Albany, Georgia: Albany Sesquicentennial Commission, 1986.

Morgret, Charles O. Brosnan. *The Railroads' Messiah*. 2 vols. New York: Vantage Press, 1996.

O'Donovan, Susan E. "Transforming Work: Slavery, Free Labor, and the Household in Southwest Georgia, 1850-1880." Ph.D. Dissertation, University of California, San Diego, 1997.

Pace, Jim B. *Memories, Tall Tales and Other Stuff*. Albany, Georgia: Privately printed, 1992-94.

AUTHOR'S NOTES:

Albany on the Flint; Indians to Industry: 1836-1946 is a delightfully told history with some of the usual problems of older, locally done works—a beautifully illustrated history of Albany written with restraint and wit. In *Glancing Backward*, Dougherty County high school students did most of the collecting of materials for the publication. Dated but accurate, the Inventory of the County Archives of Georgia is the best source on Albany's earlier history. Early chapters of *The Railroads' Messiah* include the life of D. William Brosnan, the subject's father. The elder Brosnan was the colorful city fire chief of Albany in the 1930s and later—a well done, if adoring biography that deserved a university or commercial publisher. "Transforming Work: Slavery, Free Labor, and the Household in Southwest Georgia, 1850-1880" is an exhaustive and narrowly focused dissertation, but the information is of great interest and makes absorbing reading. There is still much to be gleaned from the recollections in *History and Reminiscences of Dougherty County* on the earliest period in the county's and the city's history. It needs to be updated and republished with later reminiscences. *Memories, Tall Tales and Other Stuff*, a collection of colorful tales and characters from Albany's recent and more remote past, is a wonderful book full of local color. Part of it is true and all of it is entertaining.

Enterprises Index

Index